The Women's Giving Circle Guide

Get Together, Give Together, and Make a Difference

Caterina Rando and C.J. Hayden

THRIVE
PUBLISHING™

The Women's Giving Circle Guide: Get Together, Give Together, and Make a Difference
Copyright © 2017 Caterina Rando and C.J. Hayden

Thrive Publishing
A Division of PowerDynamics, Inc.
San Francisco, CA
www.thrivebooks.com

ISBN-10: 0-9897129-8-2

ISBN-13: 978-0-9897129-8-9

Dedicated to the generous women around the world whose giving has inspired us to "give until it feels great."

CONTENTS

INTRODUCTION

"I have found that among its other benefits,

giving liberates the soul of the giver."

—Maya Angelou, American author and activist

Several years ago, the two authors of this book were delighted to receive invitations to celebrate the birthday of spirituality author Maggie Oman Shannon. With our friend Maggie and her other women guests, we enjoyed an afternoon of sipping tea, nibbling on treats, partaking in stimulating conversations, and celebrating friendship.

Near the end of the gathering, Maggie reached for a newspaper clipping on the coffee table. "I'd like to share with everyone this piece I read about the Nepal Youth Foundation. One of their projects is the Indentured Daughters Program. They rescue young girls who have been sold into indentured servitude and send them to school. It takes only $100 for the NYF to rescue a girl. Could we all chip in and collect enough for them to rescue a girl today?"

For us, hearing Maggie's idea was a defining moment. We realized that a pleasant afternoon with friends could easily become much more than just a fun time. If we all opened our wallets and each pulled out even a small amount, we had the potential to change someone's life forever.

We didn't know it then, but what we created in Maggie's living room was a giving circle — a group of people who agree to pool their donations to an agreed-upon charitable cause.

The feeling of making such a significant difference with a small, easy gesture was so inspiring that by the time we arrived home that day, our idea for regularly getting together to give was born.

Ever since then, the two of us, with help from many others, have been raising money to empower developing world women and girls. We began using our current giving circle model in 2012. Since that time, our circle has been making a substantial impact with a relatively small amount of effort. We wrote this book to share exactly how we operate our giving circle, to inspire women like you to do the same, and to break through the barriers that keep too many women with giving hearts from making the difference that they could.

This guide will give you step-by-step advice and support to get your own giving circle started and make it thrive. We will show you how easy it is to start a giving circle, and dispel some of the myths about philanthropy that may be holding you back.

One of the biggest obstacles that prevents many women from embracing philanthropy now, rather than later, is the limiting belief that you cannot make a significant difference if you are not wealthy. This can be a huge block to philanthropic giving, because many women do not perceive themselves as having enough surplus funds to become major donors. They often tell themselves that they will start giving when they "have enough." But somehow, achieving enough wealth to become a philanthropist stays far off in the distance while the years pass.

You see grey-haired docents at the local museum, or retired volunteers at the community garden, and consciously or unconsciously, you may think that giving back mostly happens late in life, after a long career, or after the kids are off on their own. Who has the time to contribute in that way now? Or perhaps you believe that only women with high-paying jobs, trust funds, or family money are affluent enough to donate to causes in any appreciable amount. You'd like to give back, but you just don't see yourself as having enough time and money to make a real difference on an ongoing basis.

That's why we believe giving circles are the best possible avenue to turn busy women of ordinary means into philanthropists. When you gather together with others, you multiply your contributions.

At Maggie's party, any one of us alone might have only been able to give ten dollars that day. But ten contributions of ten dollars each were enough to free a girl from semi-slavery and put her in school. Imagine what it would feel like for you to know you have changed a young girl's life by writing a small check! With a giving circle, small donations add up to make a true impact.

Insight: Learning Our Impact in Human Terms

In a recent update that our Thriving Women in Business Giving Circle received from our charity partner Power of Love Foundation, we learned that the Women Entrepreneurs Program we support was directly improving the lives of over two thousand people in Lusaka, Zambia.

Our contributions enabled Power of Love to double the number of microloans made to launch new women entrepreneurs over the past year, bringing the total number of women financially supported by this program to 372. The business operated by each of these women is typically supporting a household of seven people, of which four to five are children. Most of these women are grandmothers caring for multiple children orphaned by AIDS-related deaths.

As a result of our donations, 2,600 people are now able to eat two to three meals per day, instead of just one. Children are going to school, instead of staying home because they have no shoes or uniforms. Families have been able, for the first time, to put aside small amounts of savings to prevent a temporary setback from becoming a catastrophe.

Not only are these women entrepreneurs taking better care of their families, graduates of the program formed the "Matero Women in Business" club to mentor others. Having formed a strong social network, they now share what they have learned and are helping each other to succeed.

Reports like these from our charity partners warm our hearts and uplift our spirits. Knowing our impact is truly rewarding.

This is why we love having a giving circle.

Make a Difference Right Away

A giving circle takes very little time to operate. Our circle holds a gathering only once per quarter, while our leadership team meets by phone just once per month. We have no paid staff or overhead expenses. This is quite different from what it takes to run the typical nonprofit organization. (You'll learn more about this in Chapter 1.)

With a giving circle, you don't have to wait to become a philanthropist and gain all the rewards that come from contributing to causes you care about. You can embrace philanthropy right now, and inspire others to do the same.

Women often hesitate to start a philanthropic venture because they think it will require too much energy. We are thrilled to tell you that, in this book, we have minimized the time and effort it will take you to operate a thriving giving circle. Our giving circle members and leadership team have demanding careers or run full-time businesses, while enjoying rich personal lives.

When you learn the simple approach we suggest you use for launching a giving circle, you will want to get started right away. We've made it that easy for you. Set aside some time to read each chapter carefully and take notes. We think your mind will quickly fill with ideas for what your own circle could accomplish.

Once your giving circle is up and running, we believe you will keep at it, because it will enrich your life as much as anything you have ever done. You and the women you know have the power to make a major difference in your local community or in other communities throughout the world. You have massive value to contribute to a cause you all care about. There are people waiting who want and need your help. We are honored to support you in serving the world in the way you are called to do.

Joan Baez, American singer and activist, once said: "Action is the antidote to despair." Now is the time for you to be a woman of action and invite others to act with you in changing the world.

1: GETTING STARTED WITH A GIVING CIRCLE

"Like prayers, doing charity once is not enough. You have to do it continuously, as much as possible."

—**Neelam Saxena Chandra, Indian author**

Congratulations! You're considering giving back to your community or to a cause you care about by forming a giving circle. In this book, we define a giving circle as a group of like-minded and like-hearted people who share a common concern, and who agree to pool their charitable donations to one or more agreed-upon entities. Although we are writing specifically to women, your giving circle can also include men or children.

We'll describe throughout this book how to host gatherings for your giving circle. For us, an important part of the circle we started – the Thriving Women in Business Giving Circle – is getting together as a group. Most of our gatherings are very simple, and require very little planning or expense. This is one of the many reasons we believe that giving circles are an easier approach to philanthropy than other avenues, such as holding large fundraising events.

The recipients of a giving circle's donations can be non-profit charitable organizations, and that is where most giving circle dollars go. A giving circle might also support people in your community who are in need, like a family needing financial assistance due to an accident or medical condition. Or, your circle may fund a particular project, like a new softball field at your child's school.

Your circle may decide together what causes and charities to support, or your circle may be made up of people who are already connected to a particular cause. Our giving circle operates independently of our charity partners, and we choose as a group each year who our partners will be. Other circles form with the express purpose of supporting a specific charity, church, school, or other cause.

Giving circles are typically active for many years, with some members remaining constant, and others coming and going. A giving circle might also exist for a shorter period of time to support a specific project like sending someone to college, or building a health clinic in a remote community.

The members of giving circles usually pledge to make contributions of a set amount on a regular schedule, donating monthly, quarterly, or annually. Some circles don't require pledges, allowing members, or guests at circle events, to donate varying amounts at flexible times.

Giving circles are a wonderful and unique answer to fundraising because they are so easy to form. This ease allows you to get started quickly and keep going with less effort.

In the Appendix of this book, you'll find a start-up checklist of the steps we recommend you follow in forming your circle. Share this checklist with others who are helping you get started, and check off each step as you complete it. Your giving circle will be up and running in no time.

Why Giving Circles Are the Answer

The typical giving circle requires none of the red tape and administrative responsibility that you must shoulder to start and operate a formal nonprofit. We have found that many people think carrying out sustained good work or organized giving requires launching a nonprofit. We frequently hear women ask how they can get a nonprofit started. There are thousands of people in the U.S. taking that route each year.

Unfortunately, many of them abandon their mission within a short time. Operating a nonprofit is a complex undertaking that may require too much energy and attention for those of us who already have full lives.

What nonprofit founders discover is that running a nonprofit requires operating a bank account, maintaining a budget, filing tax returns, providing donor receipts, and complying with your own group's bylaws, plus a host of state and federal regulations. Managing all of this takes not only time, but also money, which means the organization will have overhead expenses. Then additional funds must be raised just to cover administrative costs.

While for some, a nonprofit organization may be the right road to take, forming your own nonprofit is not the fast track to having significant impact. In fact, it can be a roadblock to doing anything at all. Even when desire, commitment, and enthusiasm are present in large amounts, the ongoing responsibilities of a nonprofit can smother even the hottest fire for changing the world.

We know. We initially started an all-volunteer nonprofit, but we found it to be an unrealistic path for women who also are holding down jobs, running businesses, or managing families. Running the organization itself took time and money away from our mission to serve women and girls in the developing world.

Scrapping the nonprofit was the best decision we ever made. Our giving circle doesn't even have a bank account. Our members make their donations directly to organizations we have carefully selected, which are already dedicated to carrying out our circle's mission. Now, all our attention is on fulfilling the objectives that touch our hearts, and we have more energy to put into finding new giving circle members and expressing appreciation to the members we have. Even our leadership team gets to focus on the activities they love — activities that make a real difference — instead of on accounting, compliance, and covering our costs.

Launching and running a giving circle is much simpler and easier than operating a nonprofit. In less time than it takes for a new nonprofit to file its organizing paperwork, your giving circle can be making the world a better place.

Insight: You Have the Social Capital to Build a Circle

Your social capital is the value of the people in your personal and professional network — both online and offline — who view you favorably. This means they know you, like you, and trust you. When we think favorably about someone, we want to help them. Your relationships are like currency.

Recognize that you have social capital, even if you do not hold a high paying job (or any paying job), even if you live in a small community, and even if you never went to college. If you are a friendly, kind, and gracious person, you have a network that you can use to grow your circle and have it thrive. You can tap into your network by making requests of them. After all, people cannot help you if they do not know what you need.

Social capital is not only valuable to build your giving circle, it is also valuable to gain things your circle might need: space to hold your meetings or events, volunteers to help with a website or social media page, or friends to help you prepare for a giving circle gathering. When you make use of your social capital, it is not like a bank balance where funds are reduced once you use them. You can maintain your current balance by acknowledging and thanking people personally for their help, donations, or attendance at your gatherings.

We bring up social capital because many women do not realize they have it. We women are always so focused on helping others that we often forget the many people who would be more than happy to help us.

Use your social capital to further your giving circle. On any day when you don't feel you can make a difference with your efforts, remember what anthropologist Margaret Mead said: "Never doubt that a small group of thoughtful, committed citizens can change the world. Indeed, it is the only thing that ever has."

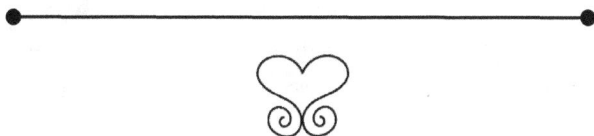

Why Get Together to Give?

You could just give on your own to causes you care about, rather than be part of a giving circle. Of course, it is always good to make donations to a worthy cause, but we think giving as a group is much more rewarding.

As part of a giving circle, your contribution is pooled together with everyone else's. As a result, the amount donated becomes more significant. Instead of feeling like the most you can give is still only a drop in the bucket, you experience the impact of your circle's total donations. A $100 donation may not seem like much. But when you add it together with nine more donations just like it, your funds can buy sewing machines for a group of deaf women in Nepal, and hire an instructor who teaches them how to sew.

Another reason to donate through a giving circle rather than on your own is that your circle can develop an intimate relationship with the causes you support. Charitable organizations don't have the resources to communicate individually with every small donor. But your giving circle can become a major donor, entitling your group to VIP status.

For the causes our giving circle supports, we established as a criterion that the recipient organizations have a strong relationship with our circle. We can always reach one of their representatives directly by phone or email, and they provide us with a report each quarter telling us exactly how our contributions were used. Even though none of the charities we support are headquartered in our region, two of them have sent a representative to attend some of our events, and one of them hosted a special webinar just for our members. At year-end, our charity partners send us a video thank-you, recorded just for our circle.

Unless you are in the top percentage of donors for an organization, a giving circle will give you much more influence with the organizations you support than an individual donor can ever expect.

Also, with a giving circle, each member knows that designated representatives of her group will check out the supported organizations in advance. (You'll learn more about that process in Chapter 3.) This allows members to be confident that their funds will be used well. It also saves them the time needed to do that research themselves.

Perhaps the best part of starting or joining a giving circle, which makes it much more enjoyable than donating directly, is that you can get to know the other awesome people in your circle. You'll know they are wonderful individuals, because, like you, they chose to be part of this effort to make the world a better place.

You can make lifelong friends, find other rewarding reasons to get together, and expand your personal and professional network. For our older members, at a time of life when many people's connections are decreasing, the members of our circle are increasing the number of like-minded people they know. Our giving circle members have exchanged recipes, gained clients, discovered new resources, and invited each other to parties, art classes, crafting events, and much more.

Plus, if you ever want to visit any of the sites where the organizations you support do their good work — whether they are across the street or across the world — you will have companions to go with. This ensures you will have a better time and will increase the likelihood of being treated like a VIP — much more so than if you visited on your own.

One more thing to consider is that when you start or join a giving circle, you encourage others to give. When you invite people to join your circle and the other circle members do the same, this exponentially increases the amount of giving. Each member's pledge to the other members of the circle motivates her to keep giving even when her funds are tighter than usual. Encouraging more giving is a key outcome created by every giving circle.

Can't You Volunteer Instead of Donating?

We encourage you to volunteer as much as it fills your heart to do so. Many of our circle members have donated their time and expertise, as well as their money, to the organizations we support. One of our members built a website for Sakhi for Girls' Education, which up until then had only a Facebook page. Three of our members helped The Rose International Fund for Children set up a store on Etsy to sell the greeting cards handmade by the Deaf Women's Empowerment Group.

So, please do volunteer. Give your time, share your expertise, and help any way you can. But know that every cause needs financial contributions as well as volunteers in order to make a significant difference. The causes you care about all need funding.

We believe that many women have a false impression when they choose to volunteer instead of donating money. They mistakenly think they are not yet wealthy enough to make financial contributions. This is where the power of a giving circle comes in. When your small contribution is added to the contributions of the other women in your circle, together, you now have a large contribution.

We want to encourage women to start giving as soon as they possibly can. It has been heartwarming to watch women come to one of our giving circle's gatherings, saying they cannot afford the pledge we require to join, and then come back later and become circle members, because they have held the aspiration of joining us. It's touching to see their faces beaming with pride and joy as they step up and become donors. Every new member in our circle fuels our desire to get every woman giving. You will see this in your circle, too, and feel an enormous satisfaction as you watch it unfold.

Get Clear on Your Commitment

If you think you're ready to get started with a giving circle of your own, we suggest you and any others involved begin by reflecting on your level of commitment. How much time you are willing to invest on a monthly basis in operating a giving circle? If you have ever volunteered for a nonprofit or community group, you already know that it can take up as much time as you can give it. There are always new projects you could start, initiatives you might expand, or things to improve.

In our giving circle, we have some truly dedicated leaders who keep the circle going strong. But we have also had women join our leadership team only to leave soon after, when they realized their circle responsibilities would require more time and attention than they were willing to give.

We suggest that you and any others involved ask yourselves:

- Are you willing to commit to leading your giving circle for at least two years (if not for many years to come)?
- Are you able to dedicate at least eight hours per month to leadership team activities, in addition to time spent attending events as a circle member yourself?

You can make your circle commitments as easy as you need to, in order to fit them into the time you have available. For example, we hold our monthly leadership team meetings virtually, on a telephone conference line. Our giving circle gathers only quarterly. When you add our annual circle member appreciation event to that, our in-person commitment only requires five days per year. We even have an agreement on our leadership team that each leader is allowed to miss one of those events each year.

This is what we have decided works for us. If all your leadership team members live in the same neighborhood, you may love to gather once per month over afternoon tea, or host an evening potluck for your team meetings.

Decide up front that you're willing to make a long-term, regular commitment to this endeavor. Then you'll be entitled to expect the same commitment of those who you choose to lead your circle along with you.

Assemble Your Organizing Team

In order to get started forming a giving circle, you'll need some capable help. We recommend you find at least two other people who are willing to serve on your organizing team. When women start a volunteer project, they often begin telling everyone they know and inviting anyone who is interested to join in. While that approach could work out, we encourage you to be more strategic.

Before you start to broadcast what you are up to, consider the type of person you want to help you with this project. We've found that the best type of women to serve on your initial organizing team will be action-oriented, share your enthusiasm about the project, and have demonstrated their ability to complete projects, keep commitments, and operate with integrity. Those are the people you want to be working with.

When you have identified two or more like-minded, like-hearted women who meet the criteria above, invite them to join you for a discussion about forming a giving circle together. When you meet, gauge their level of interest, and also assess how much they want to be involved in leadership. The people you invite to join your giving circle's initial organizing team need to be highly motivated. Sometimes we really want people to be involved, and they want to support us, but they are not committed enough to serve as leaders. Those people can be involved in other ways. For your organizing team, hold out for people who you can rely on to do their part.

The choices you make when you first get started will affect the ultimate success of your giving circle. Be judicious. Do not compromise about the level of commitment you are seeking. Committed people are the ones who get things done.

2: CREATING YOUR GIVING CIRCLE'S MISSION AND IDENTITY

"If giving to the needy makes me sleep every
night, then I will do it every day."

—Gugu Mona, South African author and poet

B efore you and your organizing team start inviting others to join you in a giving circle, you'll want to have clarity on the mission of your circle. What type of causes will your circle support? Your mission may evolve or change over time. You may gain more clarity after you have some experience with your circle. But you need to establish a shared mission to begin with, in order to attract like-minded people to join you.

Since we are recommending to you that you not form a nonprofit, but instead give directly, it's your circle's mission that will guide you in choosing the right recipients for the funds you raise.

What Should Your Mission Be?

If you are forming a circle to support a specific cause, you may already be clear on your mission. But if you're forming an independent giving circle like ours, answer the questions below, and you will be well on your way to establishing the mission for your circle.

Who or what do you want to help?

There is need everywhere. There are people all over the globe and in your local community that are all worthy of your support. Equally worthy are organizations that support the environment, wildlife, or companion animals. Your giving circle will be most successful when you choose a specific population or issue to serve. You may want to help at-risk youth, single mothers, or families who have received a cancer diagnosis. Or, you may feel called to serve foster children, illiterate adults, or military spouses who have lost their partners.

Where are the people you want to serve or the issues you want to address?

Once you know who or what you want to help, the next question is where. You may want to focus on your local community. Or, you may feel called to serve people in a country across the world, or in the rural area where you grew up. You'll need to determine your geographic range. Do you want to help people or causes in your city or town, your county, your state or province, throughout your nation, in another specific country, or around the world?

Is there a specific need, problem, or goal you want to fund?

Keep in mind that you can change the future with what you decide today. What exactly do you want the funds you raise to do? Should they pay for research, housing, nature preserves, school uniforms, or microloans? Or do you want the recipients themselves to determine how to use the funds?

When we started the Thriving Women in Business Giving Circle, we determined that our mission would be to support the education and economic empowerment of women and girls in the developing world, and that we wanted our funds directed to women's entrepreneurship and girls' education. That fairly broad mission provided us with a wide range of existing organizations to choose from, while also guiding us about what groups we should consider.

If your interest is more local, you may want to start with a small, specific focus and expand from there. For example, if you wanted to raise money for your son's high school band, you could start with raising funds for uniforms. Then once you gain more support, you could expand to add a supplement for each band member to cover their travel expenses, or even buy them a new bus.

The possibilities are endless for what you can do with the money you raise. We suggest that, in the beginning, you choose something specific for which you want to raise funds. We began by selecting just one group that was in line with our mission, which was the Nepal Youth Foundation's Indentured Daughters Program that we mention in the Introduction.

Insight: Bringing Books to Girls in the Slums of India

When the Thriving Women in Business Giving Circle first exchanged emails with Aarti Naik, founder of Sakhi for Girls' Education, we asked her this question: "If our giving circle were to begin supporting your girls' learning center in India, what would our contributions enable you to do that you aren't doing already?"

Aarti had an answer for us. She shared her vision that girls living in the slums of Mumbai would have regular access to books. She pictured a book bank, which would deliver books door-to-door to girls who could not come to the learning center. Each girl visited would receive a new book in English, Hindi, or Marathi to read every week. Older girls would deliver the books as volunteers, and this would serve them as a leadership training program. The project would also create more awareness among the girls' mothers about the importance of reading.

For us two authors, reading was an important part of our childhood. We couldn't imagine what it would be like to not have access to books. We brought Aarti's proposal to our giving circle members, and they enthusiastically voted to support Sakhi's book bank.

A few months later, Aarti emailed us a photo of a room full of smiling young girls holding a banner, which read "Girls' Book Bank: Helping Slum Girls to Read and Lead." At the bottom of the banner was the name of our giving circle as the project's sponsor. Seeing this photo brought tears to our eyes.

Today, 350 girls in Aarti's slum community are receiving a new book to read every week. Aarti says this is helping to cultivate a reading culture in the community. And it all began because a handful of women in San Francisco wrote an email.

What If Your Mission Isn't Obvious?

You may have picked up this book because you want to help others, but you do not yet have clear answers to the questions above. We understand that. Many women are happy to help anyone, any time. If you aren't sure what people or issues you most want to serve, you may be someone who has been helping others in a variety of ways for as far back as you can remember. Good for you. You are the kind of woman who will make a giving circle thrive.

You still need to make some decisions to ensure your success. We have a different set of questions for you. Reflect on each of these and write down what comes to mind.

What problems or goals inspire you the most?

Maybe you were thrilled when you found out about a program that sends low-means students to college, or you were happy to learn about a space in your community where homeless women and children can go during the day when shelters are closed. Perhaps you got excited when you were asked to be on your company's team for a fundraising walkathon for AIDS research. Take a moment and reflect on what has inspired you recently.

What types of stories or issues have, in the past, inspired you to do something?

Think over your younger life. In grade school and high school, where did you make a difference? Did you participate in a blood drive or canned goods collection? What about more recently? Did you organize all the women in your neighborhood to sign a petition to get a much-needed stop sign on a busy corner? Consider what has caused you to take action throughout your life.

What kind of impact would you like to have in your local community or in the world?

If you don't have an immediate answer to this question, then ask yourself: what is not okay with you?

Does it break your heart when you hear about a family that has lost someone to drunk driving or gang violence? The first time you heard about genital mutilation or girls being sold as indentured servants, did it ruin your whole day? Did you feel physically ill when you found out that people in the military can have their homes foreclosed on while they are on active duty in another country? Think about where you would really like to make a difference.

Is there a specific goal you want to accomplish with your giving?

By the time you have read this far, you may already know what you want to do. However, you may not yet be sure that you can actually do it. That's okay right now. First, just get clear on what you want to accomplish. It is fine for you to want what you want, even if you are not sure others will feel the same way.

Consider the ultimate goal to which you would like your giving circle to contribute. Is it economic independence for women in Malawi, finding a cure for cystic fibrosis, or college graduation for inner city youth in your town? Allow yourself to have big dreams. What you desire will inform your mission.

Write a Mission Statement for Your Circle

Your giving circle's mission statement should describe who or what you help, what people or issues you serve, and what need, problem, or goal you fund. Here are a few giving circle mission statements to inspire you.

Beehive Collective is a giving circle that awards grants to nonprofits working toward making Raleigh, North Carolina, a better place. By pooling our resources and organizing fun events, we raise money to fund causes ranging from public transportation to youth health care.

www.thebeehivecollective.org

Impact 100 Greater Indianapolis is a charitable women's giving circle dedicated to awarding high impact grants to nonprofits in our community in the areas of arts and culture, education, environment, family, and health and wellness.

www.impact100indy.org

Saffron Circle is a giving circle serving the Greater Boston Asian and Asian American community. Our members pool resources to provide critical support for nonprofits, from established organizations to emerging programs. We seek to fund initiatives that will leverage our contributions and positively impact the Asian community.

www.saffroncircle.strikingly.com

Dining for Women: Through collective giving circles, Dining for Women inspires, educates, and engages people to invest in grassroots programs that make a meaningful difference for women and girls living in extreme poverty in developing countries.

www.diningforwomen.org

Anne Arundel Women Giving Together supports initiatives that improve the quality of life for women and families in Anne Arundel County, Maryland.

www.givingtogether.org

With a mission statement for your circle in place, you and your leadership team will be clear on your direction, and ready to move forward in earnest.

What Should Your Circle Be Called?

Your giving circle will need an appropriate name. The name by which your circle is known will influence who wants to join your circle, and how your circle is perceived by others you may ask for support.

Here are some elements you may wish to consider when naming your circle, illustrated with examples of circles using these elements in their name.

Mission or cause. C.J. Hayden is the co-founder of a giving circle named "A^3: Access, Advancement, Autonomy," because that is the impact the circle wishes to create for girls and women. The "Black Women for Black Girls Giving Circle" bears that name because it's dedicated to supporting the empowerment of black girls in New York City.

Membership or affiliation. The "Cherry Blossom Giving Circle" is made up of people who wish to create positive change in the Asian American and Pacific Islander communities in the Washington, D.C. area. The "SPCA Florida Women's Giving Circle" was formed specifically to support the work of SPCA Florida.

Geographic location or focus. The "Catonsville Women's Giving Circle" was founded by women located in and around Catonsville, Maryland. The "Africa Circle" was created to pool its members' funds for the benefit of economic development projects in Africa.

Circle activities. The name of the first giving circle we two authors started was "A Good Deed Tea," because our vision was that women would gather for tea and do good deeds by writing checks. The "Traveling Giving Circle to Kenya" was organized to take a group to Kenya to give funds directly to grassroots organizations they visited in person.

As you can see, you have no shortage of options for coining a name for your giving circle. Gather your organizing team and brainstorm some possibilities.

Whatever mission and name you decide on, the giving circle you create will uplift your members and those you support. It will change lives, and maybe even save lives. You will find few things more rewarding in life than knowing that you have made a powerful difference in the lives of other human beings. Your giving circle will fill your heart, and you will find that you love yourself and your life more.

3: CHOOSING THE ORGANIZATIONS YOUR CIRCLE WILL SUPPORT

"Giving saves lives. Especially the giver's."

—Shannon Kopp, American author

Deciding which organizations your giving circle will benefit is a critical step toward building a successful circle. Unless your circle is already dedicated to supporting one specific organization, you'll need to take special care with this selection. (If you're already partnering with an organization, you can skip this chapter.)

One of the key differences between a giving circle and other forms of giving is the powerful sense of community that being part of a circle creates. When you choose to support organizations which further contribute to those feelings of affinity and connection, you strengthen your circle.

Begin with Your Mission

In Chapter 2, you chose a mission for your giving circle. Focus on that mission as you begin identifying organizations that will be the best fit for your group. Consider the types of projects that might best embody your mission in real life, practical terms. Often, a giving circle's mission could potentially be carried out in multiple ways. What are some of the different types of organizations your group could fund that would carry out your mission?

For example, if your mission was to lower high school dropout rates in your community, you might choose to support:

1. An organization that works to engage families in their children's education.

2. A group that provides mentoring and tutoring to high school kids.

3. A program to help teachers adopt active learning techniques to keep students engaged.

When we sought out organizations that the Thriving Women in Business Giving Circle (TWIBGC) would benefit, we wanted groups that would align with our mission to support the "education and economic empowerment of women and girls in the developing world." We asked ourselves what kind of projects would accomplish that mission, and also allow our members to feel connected to the work being done and be able to pinpoint the exact impact of our circle's giving.

Our conclusion was that two types of projects would serve our group best: women's entrepreneurship programs, and girls' education projects. Since many of our potential members were women entrepreneurs, that category was a natural choice. Girls' education was chosen because members of our organizing team had a passion for this cause and had supported it in the past. We also felt that women's entrepreneurship and girls' education were two causes that were strongly related to each other and would have long-term and widespread impact on local communities.

When deciding what categories of organizations would work best for your circle, also consider the level of tangible impact a particular type of organization might have. An organization with the primary purpose of educating the public and raising awareness about an issue may not have as many tangible results to report as one that provides direct service to its beneficiaries. When you can report to your circle that your contributions have sent seventy-five girls to school, or saved one hundred animals from euthanasia, it will give your members a great sense of satisfaction.

Create Criteria for Choosing Organizations

Once you begin investigating organizations your group might partner with, you may find there are dozens, or even hundreds, to choose from. Your choices will become easier if you establish some criteria for making your selection. We suggest including the following in your criteria list.

Interested in partnering with you. You want the organizations you support to be interested in your giving circle and enthusiastic about having your support. While it might seem like any group would be excited about receiving your donations, some organizations are so focused on pursuing grants or major donors that they may not have time to communicate with your circle. If they are not thrilled to partner with you, then they may not be the right match.

Must be a registered charitable nonprofit. In the U.S., there are multiple categories of nonprofits. Most giving circles choose to support nonprofits which are designated as charitable. In this guide, we use the word "charity" to refer to any cause a circle might support. Charitable U.S. nonprofits are registered with the Internal Revenue Service under the classification 501(c)(3). In Canada, charitable nonprofits are registered as such with the Canada Customs and Revenue Agency. We advise choosing only nonprofits which are registered in your home country, as that will make donating easier.

Donations must be tax-deductible. Not all donations to nonprofits are tax-deductible as charitable contributions, because not all nonprofits are considered charities. Some types of nonprofit organizations that are not eligible for tax-deductible status include: lobbying groups, social clubs, civic leagues, and labor unions. Your circle may choose not to adopt the criterion of tax-deductibility. Perhaps you want to support a non-charitable organization, or a local project that is just starting up and doesn't yet have charitable status. However, you'll typically increase contributions to your circle if donations to your chosen causes will be tax-deductible.

Established for at least two years. Choosing organizations that have been up and running for a while will increase the likelihood that your contributions will have a measurable impact.

Small enough to easily maintain a personal relationship. The best beneficiaries for giving circle contributions are organizations to which your group's donations will be significant. A large charity will often not be willing to maintain personal contact with you because your donations won't be a high enough portion of their revenue. The TWIBGC has developed the best relationships with charities whose annual budget is less than $500,000.

Willing to report regularly. Ideally, your chosen charities should make a written or video report to your circle at least once per quarter that describes how your donations were spent. We suggest you seek out organizations who are willing and able to track the impact of your group's contributions and summarize it for you on a regular basis. This is not a large demand to make, as most well-run charities regularly communicate their impact to their donors. All you will need from them is a report like the ones they already produce, which has been tailored for your circle.

Maintains low overhead. Circle members want to know that their donations were mostly used to directly further the group's mission, rather than to pay for high salaries or significant overhead expenses. Charity watchdog groups suggest that no more than 35% of a charity's revenue should be spent on overhead. While large charities need full-time, salaried staff to be properly run, small charities can often be effectively run by volunteers. For the TWIBGC, we decided that the organizations we chose to support would have no salaries paid to North American staff, while developing world staff could receive appropriate compensation.

Spends a reasonable amount on fundraising. Organizations that meet other criteria may still not be the best choice if their fundraising expenses are too high. Some organizations spend more than half of the money they raise just on the cost of fundraising. Charity evaluators suggest that an acceptable ratio of fundraising expenses to funds raised is 25%: 25 cents spent to raise one dollar. The criterion used by the TWIBGC is a fundraising ratio of no higher than 15%.

Accessible for communication. In addition to regular reporting, there will be questions that circle members or potential members will have about the charity, and there may also be questions about circle donations sent and received. You want to partner with groups that will respond within a couple of days to any inquiries. The representatives of our TWIBGC charity partners truly want to communicate with our circle members. They thank our members with an email for each donation, and some of them are connected as Facebook friends with our circle members as well.

Insight: Embracing the Power of No

In order to build your circle and serve the causes you desire, you will need to invite many people to join your circle, support it, and share about it. When you are doing it right, you will hear the word "no" often. If you don't hear "no," you may hear variations like "I don't think so," "I'm not sure this is the right match for me," or "I would love to participate at some point in the future." When you develop the ability to hear "no" over and over and not let it daunt you, you are on your way to mastering fundraising.

There is significant power in developing the ability to hear the word "no" because the sales adage "every no brings you closer to a yes" is absolutely true. If you want to add five more giving circle members, then you will likely have to ask at least ten. Getting others involved and growing a giving circle does require making many requests, and this must be a continuing focus.

There is beauty in the word "no." Hearing it or not gives you clarity on who wants to get involved, who may want to get involved in the future, and who is clearly not interested. Embrace the possibility of "no." Risk hearing "no" when you make a request, then keep asking more people until you hear a "yes."

Leaders master the ability to hear "no." The capacity to consistently ask for what you want, even when you do not think you will get it, is an important skill to acquire in philanthropy and in life. The amazing thing that happens when you master the art of making requests is that you start to get what you want more often, and with more ease. Imagine that!

Searching Out the Right Organizations

Once you have established your criteria for choosing charities, ask your organizing team to propose organizations they might recommend. Additionally, request that your team members reach out to others in their personal network for suggestions. This outreach can also open the door to later conversations with those same people about joining your circle.

To expand your search beyond organizations that your team and their contacts know about, try searching online for specific types of charities that support your circle's mission. For example, you might search for "girls' education India," "animal shelters Maine," or "homelessness Chicago."

When you have eight to ten organizations on your list of possibilities, research each charity to see how well they match your criteria. We suggest you do the following.

Review the charity's website. On a charity's website, you'll be able to determine whether the organization's mission and programs are a close match for what your circle is seeking. You'll also get a sense of how well the charity does at reporting its activities and summarizing its impact. Charities that perform these functions well are the best fit for giving circle partnerships. Additionally, you may discover whether the charity's operating philosophy fits your circle's criteria. For example, the charity may indicate it maintains low overhead by stating: "100% of donations received from private donors go toward program services" or "overhead expenses are funded by the founders."

Sometimes small or new charities have no website. If this is the case, you may not wish to dismiss these groups outright when they are otherwise a good fit. However, if you partner with them, they will need to have an online presence of some kind (like a Facebook page), so that your circle members and potential members will be able to look them up. If people can't find a group online, they will typically not be confident donating to them.

Examine the charity's GuideStar or Canada Revenue Agency listing. If the organization is a charitable nonprofit, you can learn about its finances on GuideStar.org in the U.S., or in the Canada Revenue Agency Charities Listings. In the U.S., be sure to view the charity's Form 990 for the most recent tax year. (You'll need to set up a free account with GuideStar to access these.) Form 990 is the filing a charity makes with the Internal Revenue Service. In Canada, financial information from tax filings is summarized for you by the Canada Revenue Agency. (See the "full view" for the last reporting period.) A charity's tax filings will reveal the size of their annual budget, what percentage of revenue they spend on program services vs. overhead, and how much they spend on fundraising.

Visit the charity's social media profiles. Many charities maintain Facebook pages, YouTube channels, Twitter accounts, and other social media profiles. You can usually find links to these on the charity's website. Viewing a charity's social media updates will give you a sense of the kind of reporting you might expect from the charity, and also help you learn more about its activities.

Search online for news and reviews about the charity. Search for the charity's name (in quotes, if the name is more than one word) followed by the word "review" to find online reviews that have been posted about the charity. Also search Google News (news.google.com) to find any news reports. You may not find many reviews or news reports when researching small or new charities, and that's okay. But doing this search will help you discover whether there are any "red flags," such as negative reports from other donors, or an ongoing investigation of the charity's activities.

How Many Organizations to Choose

You may discover that there are numerous organizations that fit all your circle's criteria. However, resist the temptation to offer your members a long list of charities to which they might give. When you first begin, we recommend that you choose no more than three charities to which circle members will be invited to donate. Selecting just one or two would be fine.

By keeping the number of charities small, you can maximize your circle's contributions to each organization. This will help you build stronger relationships with your charity partners. Also, you will make it easier for your members to give by reducing the number of choices they have to make.

Once your circle is larger and well established, you may choose to add a fourth or fifth charity. Keep in mind that this will significantly impact how much each group receives. We suggest you not add additional charities unless your initial choices are well funded for the present and future.

Reaching Out to Potential Charity Partners

Once your research has helped you narrow the field of possible organizations to only four or five choices, contact each of your finalists personally about becoming one of your circle's charity partners. You might start with an email describing your new circle and its mission. Ask to schedule a phone call with a leader of the organization to discuss a possible giving relationship.

Charity leaders are busy, so it may take you a couple of attempts to reach the right person and schedule a conversation. But don't leave this step out and just start giving to an organization without speaking to one of its leaders first. An organization that doesn't have the time or interest to speak with a potential large donor will likely not be a good choice for your circle's giving.

In your first conversation with the charity, describe what you have in mind for your circle. Explain that your group is new, so you can't yet estimate the level of donations you might be able to give, but you are hopeful that your membership and giving ability will grow over time as your circle grows. Ask if the charity is willing to report back to your group at least quarterly about how circle donations were spent. If you followed our advice above, and are targeting small charities to begin with, you will probably find that they are eager to develop relationships like the one you are proposing.

You may find it easy to choose among your finalists after speaking with each of them. But if not, summarize what you've learned about them for the members of your organizing team, then take a vote.

As Your Circle Grows

We suggest developing long-term relationships with your charities, rather than switching to new charities each quarter or year. You'll see the impact of your circle increase as time passes. You may also find opportunities to deepen the relationship in ways other than giving money.

One of the TWIBGC's charity partners — TRIFC's Deaf Women's Empowerment Group in Nepal — produces handmade greeting cards which are embroidered by the women the charity supports. When the charity let us know they were eager to fill custom orders, we gathered together multiple TWIBGC members who were interested in purchasing thank-you cards, and placed a special order for 200 custom-made cards. Later on, one of our circle members placed a custom order for 100 cards with her company's logo embroidered on them. These sales not only helped the charity increase their income, they also enabled them to reach new supporters when we used the cards and the recipients found out where they came from.

Many charity partnerships work out quite well from the beginning. If some area of your relationship with a charity isn't turning out as you had hoped, let the charity know — tactfully — how they could improve. But don't be afraid to end one relationship and start a new one if the partnership isn't a good fit. There are many deserving organizations in the world for your circle to choose from.

We suggest that you ask your circle members to vote each year on whether to keep donating to the same charities or to choose new ones. If one of your charity partnerships doesn't seem to be working, ask your members what new charities they might recommend. Even if you decide to keep the same charity partnerships year after year, it will help keep your circle members engaged and enthusiastic if they have an ongoing say about which charities your circle will support.

4: DEVELOPING YOUR CIRCLE'S LEADERSHIP TEAM

"All of us want to do well. But if we do not do good, too,

then doing well will never be enough."

— **Anna Quindlen, American journalist**

I f you follow our advice in Chapter 1, you'll begin by putting together an initial organizing team, even if this is just you and a friend or two. Before you start inviting members to join your circle, it's a good idea to create a stronger leadership structure. Even though operating a giving circle takes less work than running other types of charitable organizations, there are still ongoing responsibilities that need attention. Dividing these duties among several people will make your circle easier and less stressful to operate. You'll also gain the benefit of the skills and connections that others who join your team will bring with them.

How to Select the Best Circle Leaders

We suggest you begin developing your leadership team by choosing some criteria you would like potential leaders of your circle to meet. Here are some examples.

Have skills your circle needs. You'll need a variety of skills among your circle leaders to manage all the tasks of operating your circle. See the next section for some of the leadership roles you may want to have filled. Be sure to look for leaders who have skills your current team may be missing.

Have a large network of potential circle members they will invite to join. The majority of your circle members will most likely join because of personal invitations extended by circle leaders. Inviting people with extensive networks to be leaders will expand your circle's reach. Although we recommend that most of your giving circle leaders meet this criterion, you might make some exceptions. For example, women who have excellent skills in certain areas, such as financial management or public relations, might be perfect candidates to fill specific roles even if they don't have a large personal network.

Are reliable, responsible, and trustworthy. Your circle leaders must be women of integrity, who are well thought of in your community. You want your leaders to be people who can be relied on to keep their commitments, and who others will be willing to trust.

Have a positive, proactive attitude. Running your circle will be more enjoyable to you, and participating will be more fun for your circle members, if your leaders possess an encouraging, constructive outlook. Graciousness, kindness, and thoughtfulness are traits that will go far to serve your leadership team and your circle. You want to have leaders that people like to be around.

Are willing to host circle gatherings. You'll need dependable volunteers to host your first few circle events. To make this easier to accomplish, seek out leaders who are willing to be event hosts, whether the gatherings take place in their homes or elsewhere. In the Thriving Women in Business Giving Circle, we request that those on our leadership team host or co-host a circle event each year. (You'll learn more about hosting circle gatherings in Chapter 7.)

Will commit for at least one year. High turnover in your leadership will hamper your circle's growth, and dampen the enthusiasm of your members. Look for leaders who are willing to make a one-year commitment to the role you are asking them to play.

Keep in mind that the best candidates for becoming leaders of your circle will be women who already have very full lives. There's a saying in the world of volunteerism that we have found to be true: "busy women get things done." Don't avoid asking someone to join your leadership team just because she seems to have a lot on her plate already. Women who make many commitments — and keep them — are likely to be the very people you need to lead your circle.

Women with a lot of commitments are often quite good at managing multiple priorities, and may have a team or staff that supports them. If you would like someone to be on your leadership team, do not assume she is too busy — ask.

Insight: Failing Forward

Since we first launched our giving circle, we have learned much about topics like philanthropy, fundraising, producing events, enrollment, and keeping members engaged. One area where we have learned a great deal is that of choosing your leadership team. We want to help you avoid our rookie mistakes.

In the beginning, we were so eager for anyone's help that we took whatever assistance they offered. As our circle matured, we discovered how tough it can be to keep volunteers motivated and on track. Here are some things we suggest you do from the outset to ensure success down the road.

Have clear criteria, in writing. Write down your expectations of what you are asking from leadership team members. That way they'll know from the start what will be involved. There will be no surprises and team members will realize exactly what they are signing up for.

Only embrace those who are all in. Never try to persuade someone who is reluctant to join your leadership team. Don't take on a team member who is overly concerned about the time commitment. You want team members who are 100% committed to making your giving circle thrive, and are happy and honored to take the time needed to get the job done.

Make every team member responsible for enrollment. We encountered some leadership team members who wanted to serve on the team just for the prestige. They were happy to show up at gatherings and be acknowledged as a circle leader, but they didn't invite any new people to join our circle. Every leadership team member must consistently invite potential new members to join the circle and attend circle events. Your giving circle won't survive long if only a couple of people are doing all the inviting.

No one is doing you a favor by taking a leadership team position. It is a privilege to serve on your team. To create a committed and engaged leadership team, be selective about who you choose.

Defining Roles on Your Leadership Team

You will want to define specific roles to be filled on your leadership team, so that certain tasks can be carried out by the same person on a regular basis. One person might hold more than one of these jobs, especially when your circle is first getting started. Below is a description of each leadership role you may wish to define. In the Appendix, we've provided sample job descriptions for each of these roles.

Circle chair. The chair of your circle holds the vision of what your group wants to accomplish and where your circle is headed. The chair is often the person who had the initial idea to get the circle started. She facilitates your leadership team's meetings, creates the agenda for those meetings, makes sure all tasks that need to be accomplished are assigned to a member of the team, and follows up with team members to make sure those tasks are completed. The chair also typically designs the program for each circle gathering. When a leadership team member isn't fulfilling her responsibilities, it's the chair who will communicate with her about this, and if necessary, ask her to step down.

Co-chair or vice-chair. Your circle might have two chairs who serve together as co-chairs, or it might have a vice chair. The vice-chair's job is to fill in for the chair when she is absent, and assist the chair with creating agendas and making sure tasks are assigned and completed.

Treasurer. The treasurer collects donations from circle members and guests at each circle event, records them, and sends them to your chosen charities. If your circle members are required to make donations whether or not they attend an event (we recommend this policy), the treasurer also follows up with circle members who are absent to secure their donation. The treasurer keeps a record of all donations made, and reports on donation totals periodically to the leadership team and circle members.

Secretary. It's the secretary's job to take minutes at your leadership team meetings and send the minutes to all team members. She also sends out email reminders for the leadership team meetings, and maintains the event and project calendar for your group. Your secretary additionally keeps a roster with contact information for circle members and leadership team members. If your group has an email address or voice mail number, your secretary is typically the person who responds to messages your group receives or forwards them to the appropriate team member.

Charity liaison. Your circle's charity liaison leads the effort to identify potential charities for your group's giving, performs a due diligence review of each charity, and organizes voting on charities by your circle members. She obtains updates from the charities your circle supports, presents the updates at circle gatherings, and circulates them to circle members. She serves as the contact point between your circle and your supported charities for any needs or questions your circle has.

Membership chair. The membership chair is responsible for inviting and cultivating new members for your circle, and for welcoming and thanking all attendees at each of your events. She also keeps in touch with current circle members, encouraging them to attend each event, and bring guests. Your membership chair may additionally be the person who arranges for circle members to host or co-host each circle gathering and ensures each hostess is well prepared to host a successful event.

PR/marketing chair. Your circle's PR/marketing chair organizes marketing, public relations, and social media activities to help promote your circle's events and raise awareness about your circle. Although we don't recommend that you spend much time promoting your circle to the public, most circles develop an audience of prospective members who they want to keep informed, and keep inviting. Plus, you'll want to keep your circle members up-to-date about your activities, and give your members tools to use for inviting friends and colleagues.

The PR/marketing chair creates flyers or social media images for your gatherings, maintains a mailing list of people interested in your events, and designs and sends event invitations. If your circle has a website or social media profile, she is responsible for designing and maintaining your site and profile, or posting to social media on your circle's behalf. She also takes photos or recruits others to do so at each of your gatherings, and uses the photos to promote your circle's activities.

Member at large. You may have a woman who is enthusiastic about getting involved, but you do not have a specific role that suits her available at the time. You can invite her to be a member at large on your leadership team, which means that she helps the other team members fill their roles, and fills in if someone is on vacation or cannot attend an event. If someone wants to do more than just be a circle member, try to find a way to involve her. Making her a member at large on the leadership team may be the ideal solution.

What to Ask of Your Leadership Team

In addition to the specific responsibilities of each role, we suggest you also set some expectations for your leadership team about how to serve as positive role models for your circle members. Below is what we ask of our circle leaders:

- Keep confidential all information shared in leadership meetings and learned about circle members.

- Speak only positively about our circle and other circle members and leaders.

- Remain in good standing as a circle member, making all promised contributions on time.

- Attend all circle events (one absence allowed per year).

- Arrive one hour early for all circle events to help set up, have a pre-event meeting with the team, and welcome guests as they arrive.

- Attend all leadership team meetings (an occasional absence is okay).

- Host or co-host a circle gathering once per year.

- Be loud and proud about our circle, personally inviting many people to each of our events.

- Promote our circle by sharing information about it in other networks or through social media.

Who to Invite as a Leader

The women you invite to join your leadership team don't have to be members of your circle already, or your personal friends. They may be work or business colleagues, neighbors, members of a club or church you belong to, retired women, or women in your community that you admire. If there's a woman you know of who you think would be a good fit, ask her if she's interested. You may be surprised at who says "yes."

Choose women that you want to work closely with, who you respect, and want to get to know better. Don't accept just anyone who shows interest. It's better to leave a position open until the right person comes along than it is to accept someone you don't have a good feeling about. Reserve the privilege of serving as a circle leader for those women who have the skills, attitude, and reputation your circle needs.

5: WORKING WITH YOUR LEADERSHIP TEAM

"It's not that successful people are givers;

it is that givers are successful people."

—Patti Thor, American author

O nce you have a leadership team in place, you'll want to design how your team will work together. Most leadership teams schedule regular meetings, and communicate in between meetings by email and sharing documents.

How to Meet with Your Team

Your team members will have rich and full lives. While it can be rewarding to get together in person, virtual meetings will garner better attendance and prevent members from feeling taxed by the time it takes to travel to meetings. You might hold your first team meeting in person so team members can get to know each other. After that, we suggest you meet via teleconference or video conference.

Free platforms where you can meet by phone include FreeConference.com and FreeConferenceCall.com. For video conferencing, you can use free platforms like Skype or Google Hangouts. Of course, you can always schedule an occasional meeting in person, if you like.

In the very beginning, you'll probably want to meet every couple of weeks. Once you get rolling, a monthly meeting should be enough, except just before or after a circle event, when you might want to meet more often.

Our virtual meetings are typically an hour long. In-person meetings work better if you allow at least ninety minutes.

What Happens in Team Meetings

We recommend that your chair put together the agenda for each team meeting, and email it to the team a couple of days before the meeting date. That will allow individual team members time to suggest topics they might want to bring up as "other business."

Try to begin and end each meeting with an upbeat tone. You may want to ask each team member to check in briefly at the beginning of the meeting by sharing a recent success. Then have the chair conclude the meeting by thanking everyone for their ongoing participation and enthusiasm, and expressing excitement about the group's next steps.

A typical agenda for a leadership team meeting looks like this:

- A quick check-in and sharing of a recent success from each member
- Review the previous meeting's minutes
- Debrief your last event
- Plan your next event
  - Date and location
  - Host and co-hosts
  - Food and drink
  - Special guests or program

- Audiovisual setup
- RSVPs so far; setting a goal for RSVPs
- PR/marketing chair's report
  - Promotion/invitation plans for your next event
- Membership chair's report
  - New members since your last meeting
- Treasurer's report
  - New contributions since last meeting
  - Total contributions made to date
- Other business suggested by any team member
- Date and time for next team meeting

Have your secretary take minutes at each meeting and distribute them to team members not present. You may also want to record your meetings, which is easy to do on any teleconference or video conference platform. That way any team member who missed the meeting can review the recording.

When you make plans in a team meeting, be sure to assign each needed task to a specific person, and give her a due date to complete it. Ask your secretary to take notes about these assignments, so that everyone on the team is clear about what should happen next.

Insight: Contribution Develops Leadership

One of the wonderful things that happens when you lead a giving circle is that you also improve your leadership skills. Once you launch a giving circle, you will be called on to expand your skills in order for your circle to succeed. Here are three skills you will likely find yourself improving.

Public speaking is something many people avoid. We encourage our leadership team members and circle members to begin speaking publicly with easy responsibilities, like making announcements or introducing someone. When members are successful at small public speaking tasks, they will be ready to take on bigger speaking opportunities. When a circle member flourishes with public speaking after previously avoiding it, her overall confidence grows as well.

Enrollment is the skill of inviting people to participate in an activity in such a way that makes them want to be part of it. In your circle, you'll be inviting people to join your leadership team, attend an event, host an event, join your circle, etc. Successful enrollment requires expressing positivity, enthusiasm, and confidence in your requests. Once you develop this leadership skill, asking for — and getting — what you want elsewhere in your life will become easier.

Acknowledgment — showing our appreciation to others for their contribution — is a skill that many of us are never taught. See Chapter 9 for suggestions on how to develop this skill. Improving your acknowledgment skills will increase your leadership ability, as you will be better able to let people know that their contribution is seen and appreciated. The rewarding thing about improving your skill at acknowledgment is that it will enhance your career and personal relationships as well.

Starting a giving circle will enhance your life in many ways. Developing your leadership skills is one more benefit of contributing your time and effort to make the world a better place.

Outside Your Team Meetings

Find a way to communicate with all of your leadership team members outside of meetings that works for everyone. Many teams use email for this, but for a group of women with overloaded inboxes, you might choose to use Facebook messages, texts, a messaging app, or some other channel that everyone will pay attention to.

Have your secretary create a roster of your team members that includes everyone's complete contact information, so it's easy to stay in touch.

You'll also want to set up an online area where documents can be shared among your team members, such as Dropbox or Google Drive.

Tips for Working with Your Team

If you followed our advice in Chapter 4, you've developed job descriptions for each member of your team. You'll want to give each team member a copy of her job description, and make sure she understands everything that's on it. Ask for her agreement to fulfill those responsibilities without having to be reminded. Here are some other suggestions for making your leadership team run smoothly.

Your team will get more done if you make sure that each person knows at the end of every team meeting what she is supposed to do next, and you establish deadlines for every task.

When you have a lot going on, consider creating a project schedule listing all the needed tasks, along with who is responsible for each, and the due dates. You can ask your secretary to keep this current, or store the document in the cloud and have each person update it as tasks are completed.

Even when you have structures like the above in place, team members won't always accomplish what's expected of them on a timely basis. Your group's chair or co-chair will typically need to follow up with team members periodically to keep them on track.

When members don't complete their assigned tasks, be considerate of their other responsibilities, but don't let "I was too busy" become your team's mantra. Your circle can have a powerful impact on the world, which increases with every new member or successful event. Our circle raised $44,000 one year, and as a result, women in Africa were able to feed their families, girls in India could stay in school, and hearing-impaired women in Nepal reclaimed a place in their community. Keep reminding your team members of the impact their work can have on the causes you support.

Acknowledge your team members often for all the effort they put into the group. In Chapter 9, we'll share some specific ways you can show appreciation to your team members and circle members, but a simple thank you every time you interact with a team member will help keep them motivated.

Sometimes a team member doesn't seem to be working out. This can be because she isn't doing her job, she's having personality clashes with others on the team, she's not communicating well, or she appears to be headed in a different direction than the rest of you. First, take some time to acknowledge the good things she has done for the group, then let her know how she could do a better job. Allow her some time to improve her performance.

When a team member doesn't improve enough to become a welcome and productive member of the team, you may find it necessary to ask her to step down. Don't avoid doing this because you aren't sure how you will replace her. It's more important to have a team that works well together than it is to have every job filled at all times. When your team members enjoy their time working together, they will naturally attract others who will be a good fit.

Your team members won't always agree on every issue. Decide whether you will use majority rule to make decisions, or insist on having everyone agree. If you want all decisions to be unanimous, you may each have to compromise to find a place of agreement.

Working with a Team Is Both Challenging and Rewarding

There's no question that your circle will have a greater impact when it has an effective leadership team in place. If you typically work on projects alone, it may be challenging to make the transition to working with a team. You'll see that it's worth the effort, though, when you see how much more your circle can accomplish with multiple team members pulling in the same direction.

You may also find, as we have, that working together as a giving circle leadership team will deepen your relationships with the other women involved. Your team can become a supportive community of girlfriends that contribute not just to the world, but to each other.

6: FORMING YOUR CIRCLE'S MEMBERSHIP

"No one has ever become poor by giving."

—Anne Frank, German-born diarist

With your giving circle's mission, charity partners, and leadership team in place, you're ready to start attracting more members. Your leadership team will be the core membership of your circle, so by designating leaders first, you already have a head start on forming your circle.

Who Will Your Members Be?

Your leadership team needs to decide the standards for membership in your circle. You'll want to agree among you on the best criteria for attracting other like-minded people with the ability to contribute. Consider who will be the most enjoyable members for you to spend time with, and what profile might create the most cohesion within the group.

Will your circle membership…

Include women only? Women and men? Children? In our circle, we limit membership to adult women, but some giving circles have men or children as members.

Allow couples or families to have a joint membership? Our circle allows women with same-sex spouses to join as a couple, requiring only a single contribution from the two. We also allow mothers and daughters to join as a family, so long as the daughters are at least twelve years old.

Be restricted to a geographic area? Our circle serves only our local area, as we hold all our events in person. Some circles choose to meet virtually, and collect contributions online from far-flung members.

Be members of certain professions? If you and many of your friends are nurses, for example, you could choose to attract other nurses as members. Your definition of the profession your circle serves could be narrow and specific, like "teachers," or broader and more open, such as "women in technology."

Share an affinity? Giving circles often are formed by women who share a religion or church, belong to the same association or club, or have attended the same school. If your circle is being formed to support one specific charity, you might require that prospective circle members be affiliated with that charity as members or alumni.

How Much Should Each Member Give?

Some circles allow members to give any amount they wish. We think it works better to establish a minimum level of giving and ask each member to pledge at least that amount. This will provide your circle with a predictable flow of contributions, which in turn, will enable stronger relationships with the charities you support. Setting a minimum will also encourage some members to contribute more than perhaps they otherwise might. In addition, it avoids feelings of competition or envy within the circle, which can arise when some members give much more than others.

In the Thriving Women in Business Giving Circle, we ask that each member meet the minimum. We thank everyone equally for giving. If a member gives a more substantial contribution, we don't make that public.

In our circle, we ask each member to give $1,000 per year, which can be paid by the quarter or even by the month. This works out to only $83.33 per month, which for many women is less than they spend on coffee, manicures, and other incidentals that contribute much less to the wellbeing of the world. Other giving circles we've seen establish minimums that range from just a few dollars per year up to many thousands.

We've based our minimum pledge on a yearly contribution rather than an amount to be paid at each event, and suggest that you do the same. Requiring an annual contribution encourages more continuity in the membership. There are always members who have to miss gatherings, and with an annual pledge, we still expect them to contribute. This does mean, though, that our group has to have a system for collecting pledges from absent members. See Chapter 8 for more details.

Choose a minimum amount that you believe will be a good match with the type of members you want to have. Don't think that you need to set your minimum low to attract more members. Instead, think about what amount might attract *committed* members. That's who you want in your group.

When and Where Will Your Group Gather?

To start inviting members, you'll need to decide when and where your group will get together. Some giving circles meet monthly, others bi-monthly, and a few only meet once per year. We chose quarterly meetings for our circle. That felt to us like the right frequency for the busy women who we imagined as members.

Giving circles that meet in person, like ours does, typically meet in members' homes or a local restaurant or café. If your circle is made up of members from an affinity group, you may have other choices available, such as the church or school your members are affiliated with.

When there's a cost involved in obtaining the meeting place or providing food and drink, members may decide to either split this evenly among themselves, or take turns picking up the cost. For example, if you're meeting in a member's home, she may supply all the refreshments. Then your next gathering could take place at another member's home, and that member would provide food and drink. If you meet at a restaurant or café, each member might pay her own check, or groups of members might take turns paying the expenses for everyone.

Deciding how to handle hosting responsibilities and costs when you first get started will allow you to make regular hosting or co-hosting a requirement of membership. We ask our circle's members to agree to host or co-host at least once every other year. Typically, the host holds the gathering at her home, while co-hosts bring refreshments or share expenses. We occasionally meet at a restaurant or café, and in that case, a group of co-hosts pick up the check for the whole group.

Insight: Expand Your Circle and Soar

To ensure the long-term success of your circle, it will be important to constantly be on the lookout for new members. Here are some things we have learned that will support you in enrolling new members into your circle.

Advance planning. Setting the dates for your giving circle gatherings well in advance helps potential guests add the future dates to their calendar early, so they can come see what you are up to. We create a flyer showing the dates of our events for the entire year, and make it available to all our members. We have seen that it may take several invitations over a period of months before someone attends an event and joins our circle.

Spread the word. When you strike up a conversation with someone who is a likely candidate for your circle, remember to invite her to attend. Keep your circle on your short list of topics to discuss when you meet people. Caterina recalls running into a woman she knew at an event and telling her about our giving circle. The woman had just broken ties with a charitable organization that was going in a direction she did not agree with, and was looking for a new place to participate in giving. She soon joined our circle.

Encourage your hosts to heavily invite guests. We have had much success with people joining our circle when they come to a gathering because they are friends of the hostess. Make sure your hostesses pay more attention to the guest list, and less attention to the snacks, for all in-home gatherings. Our best source of new members has been hostesses who invited many people to a gathering in their home.

Put everyone in the circle on the "membership committee." Create a culture where every circle member consistently supports the circle by inviting new potential members to become a part of the great work you are doing.

Identify and Invite Members

When you've made all the decisions above, write them out in the form of a description of your group that includes membership requirements. (See the example in the Appendix.)

Then create a wish list of potential members made up of people your organizing team personally knows. This is the best place to start for your first group of members. People who know you are much more likely to respond to your invitation and hopefully, come to your first gathering.

Divide up your wish list, and have each member of your organizing team extend personal invitations to the potential members she knows. Reach out to your potential members using whatever channel you believe they'll pay attention to. You might phone, email, send a text, start a Facebook chat, or plan to discuss it in person the next time you meet. (See the Appendix for a sample personal invitation.)

When you connect with a potential member, share your personal story of why you decided to become part of a giving circle, and talk about the kind of impact giving circles are making all over North America. (See the Recommended Resources in the Appendix for some ideas.) Let potential members hear your passion and enthusiasm for making a difference in this powerful way.

Don't be afraid to follow up a second or third time with potential members you don't hear back from. Most of the women we know lead rich and full lives, and can easily miss an email or voice mail, or forget to reply, even when they might be very interested in your circle. A potential circle member may have to be invited several times before she responds or attends an event.

When a woman is interested in joining, get her commitment to attend your first (or next) gathering. Then be sure to remind her of all the meeting details a few days before.

At your gathering, ask new members to make their first contribution, and commit to your membership requirements, by filling out a membership/contribution form. (See the Appendix for an example.) Recognize that some women will attend because they are curious, but may not join right away. You can still invite them to make a one-time contribution and join your group's mailing list for future events (our sample form includes those options). Perhaps they will decide to join at a later time. We have found that some women set themselves a goal of joining our circle, then become members months after they first attended as a guest.

For this reason, we place no restrictions on how many times a woman may attend as a guest without joining. Guests are always welcome to attend our gatherings and give what they can.

Welcoming New Members

When a new woman decides to join your circle, make her feel welcome and appreciated. Here's what we do to include new members when they come on board:

- Circle chair or membership chair makes a welcome call to thank her for joining the circle and answer any questions she has.

- Chair or membership chair brings a small gift to the next event to publicly acknowledge her, thank her for joining, and recognize her commitment to the circle.PR/marketing chair adds the new member's name to the list of members on the giving circle's website, Facebook page, or other online presence.

- Membership chair contacts her to arrange when she will host or co-host her first gathering.

- Treasurer sends her an acknowledgment for her first donation, which reminds her of the amount she has pledged to give and how often.

- PR/marketing chair or membership chair makes her a special member name tag to wear at future gatherings.

- Secretary adds her name to the member roster and mailing list.

- PR/marketing chair welcomes her on social media, tagging her so she'll be sure to see it, and inviting her to like/follow the circle's social media account.

Adding to Your Membership

While your first group of members will almost certainly be made up of women your organizing team already knows, it's likely you'll want to go beyond your own network over time. We initially thought that we'd cap our membership at twenty, because that seemed like the maximum number that could comfortably gather in each other's homes or around a restaurant table. But then we found that not every member attended each time, so we raised our membership cap to thirty. This was when it became important to reach out to new women.

Over time, you may find that some circle members continue to give regularly and remain committed to your circle, while not showing up at gatherings as often. This may encourage you to increase the size of your circle even more. Some members will stay with you for as long as your circle continues. Other members will stay for only a year or two. Discuss with your leadership team how big you want your circle's membership to become.

Your best source of new members will be invitations extended by your existing members. To expand your circle, ask every member to bring at least one guest to each gathering she attends. Since not everyone who attends as a guest will join, you'll likely need more prospective members than you think.

We don't recommend trying to advertise your circle or its gatherings to the public by way of event calendars or other types of general promotion. If your circle is affiliated with an existing organization, you might invite participation from that group's mailing list, website visitors, or event attendees. But with an independently organized circle, our experience has been that all of our new members have joined as the result of a personal invitation from an existing member.

We find that public promotion can take a considerable amount of volunteer time and not result in any additional members. You might also inadvertently violate state/province or local regulations about public fundraising.

Instead of reaching out to strangers, ask all your members to keep the circle in the forefront of their mind when they meet a new woman or re-connect with an old friend. Have them invite new or renewed contacts to attend your next gathering. Remind them that they may need to extend these invitations more than once.

It's a good idea to create a mailing list that includes both members and potential members, so you can send out announcements and reminders about your gatherings and other news. (See the Appendix for a sample email announcement.) For event invitations, you can use Eventbrite or Evite, but you may also want to use your mailing list for other announcements, like updates from the charities you support. We use Constant Contact for our list; another good choice would be MailChimp.

We also create a printed flyer for each gathering that we make available to our members, so they can easily share information about our circle with women they see in person. (A sample is in the Appendix.)

You can also use social media to raise the visibility of your group, since this is how many people stay connected with those they already know. Ask members to post photos of your gatherings on social media, tagging each other. If members additionally post status updates or check-ins when they attend gatherings, it will keep their online network aware of their involvement.

You might decide to set up a social media account just for your circle, to make sharing by your members easier. Our circle has a Facebook page, which we update regularly with photos from our gatherings, news from the charities we support, and invitations to our events.

Keep personally inviting new people to join you, even when you think your circle is approaching the maximum number of members you'd like to have. Every circle has some level of attrition when members decide to depart due to changes in their lives, such as leaving the area or going back to school. By continuing to reach out to potential new members, you'll always have a strong membership. This will ensure that your giving circle thrives, and continues to serve the causes you care about for many years to come.

7: HOSTING A SUCCESSFUL GATHERING EVERY TIME

"It is more rewarding to watch money change the world

than to watch it accumulate."

—Gloria Steinem, American journalist and feminist

Gatherings are essential to the success of your giving circle for several reasons. For some members, the gatherings will be one of the primary reasons they decide to join. Your members will appreciate the opportunity to connect with each other, and will build connections with other circle members. Friendships will form, resources will be shared, and support will be extended to members in need. All of this strengthens your circle.

Additionally, circle gatherings are one of the best ways to introduce potential members to your giving circle. When new people attend, you invite them to join, expanding your circle.

Hosting regular gatherings will ensure that your members stay active and present in your circle. These get-togethers can also keep members informed about where their donations are going, and the important work that is being done as a result.

Some circles consider keeping members informed about the causes they support to be a significant part of their mission. Sharing the impact your circle's donations are making gives members a great feeling, which will have them continue to rave about the circle and invite others to attend.

We know that some giving circles exist only online, as virtual communities. A circle like this is outside our experience, so we won't make recommendations about how to operate one. Our philosophy about giving circles is that they are a place to make human-to-human connections, as well as a place to give.

Below are our suggestions to ensure you have a successful gathering every time.

What Type of Gathering to Host

There are typically two different kinds of giving circle gatherings:

1. The **private gathering** is a giving circle event hosted in a member's home or place of business, or at a school or church with which your circle is affiliated. Food, beverages, and decor are provided by the designated hostesses for that gathering.

2. The **public location gathering** is a giving circle event hosted at a location such as a restaurant or tea parlor that provides the food and beverages. Either the designated hostesses split the cost of this gathering, or each attendee pays a share.

In the Thriving Women in Business Giving Circle, we schedule both kinds of events. We think gathering in someone's home creates more of a sense of community and collaboration, with co-hostesses coming early to help, and bringing their favorite dishes to share. Still, we recognize that some of our members would rather write a check than stay up late the night before, whipping up chicken salad. Having at least one event per year at a public location allows each circle member to take her turn as a hostess, without having to take time to bake or cook.

Why to Share Roles and Responsibilities

As you read this chapter, you'll notice we talk about several ways you can involve members at each gathering. We have found that the more engagement you can have from all your circle members, the more they will truly feel a part of the group. This will make them more likely to stay on as members, and give them a sense of ownership for the giving circle. It encourages each member to be an advocate and a voice for the giving circle in the rest of her life.

As you are planning your gatherings, try to give as many people as possible roles and responsibilities that they can carry out successfully, so they will happily continue to serve the giving circle.

Insight: Sharing Our Skills as Well as Our Dollars

As our giving circle has gotten to know our charity partners better, we've discovered they have other needs we can help with.

When we first started supporting Sakhi for Girls' Education in India, they had a Facebook page, but no website. Sakhi asked if our circle could help. One of our circle members, Tammy Tribble of Mimetic Design, creates websites for her clients. Tammy stepped forward to build a beautiful website for Sakhi at no cost. Now Sakhi is able to accept donations online and attract far-flung supporters for their work.

Our charity partner TRIFC, who operates the Deaf Women's Empowerment Group in Nepal, let us know they wanted to set up an online store on Etsy to sell their hand-embroidered greeting cards. Circle members Kariz Matic, Stephie Zuendorf, and C.J. Hayden all pitched in to create an Etsy store for TRIFC, complete with custom graphics. As a result, these cards are now available online for anyone to purchase, increasing income and visibility for the charity.

These are examples of how the relationship with your circle's charity partners can deepen over time, and make your circle members feel even more connected to where their dollars are going. It's so gratifying to see firsthand — as a volunteer as well as a donor — how much of a difference our time and money can make.

Help Your Hostesses Succeed

The most important thing you can do to help a hostess hold a successful gathering is make sure she doesn't have to do it alone. Whenever we have a giving circle gathering, we name a lead hostess and recruit two to four additional hostesses. The lead hostess is either a leadership team member or someone who has hosted before. She is not necessarily the person who is hosting the event in her home.

The lead hostess is responsible for making sure all co-hostesses are clear on what it takes to hold a successful gathering, and that all the necessary elements are in place.

To ensure that our hostesses are successful, we created a document called "How to Be a Great Giving Circle Hostess," which we share with our hostesses before they begin planning their gathering. This document is in the Appendix. Here are a few of the key success tips we discuss with our hostesses to ensure a successful gathering every time.

Tell guests to save the date. As soon as you know you will be a hostess, start to share the date. List who you plan to invite to this gathering, and ask your guests to save the date, even if it is several months in advance. With today's full lives, we find that the sooner guests put the gathering on their schedule, the more likely they are to attend. Your own friends and associates will often be *most* likely to attend a circle gathering when you are the one hosting, so take full advantage of this opportunity to invite them.

Invite more than you think. We find that many hostesses worry about having enough room for everyone, and hold down the number of invitations they make. We suggest you do just the opposite. Anywhere from twenty to fifty percent of the women who RSVP for an event will not show up. Life will inevitably interrupt the plans of some of those who were planning to attend. You need a good turnout at each gathering to keep your circle members excited, and inspire new people to join.

Use personal invitations more than promotion. In this age of social media, it is wonderful to post about a gathering, and have hundreds of people see your update. While this serves to make your online friends aware of your gathering, it will not fill your event, because no one feels personally invited. To have people show up for your gathering, you must personally invite them. A call, a personal email, or a one-to-one message via text or social media is much more likely to do the trick. (There are more details on how to fill gatherings in Chapter 6.)

Share that this is a giving circle event. When inviting people to attend, be sure you make clear that this is a gathering of the giving circle that you belong to. Explain that this is a fundraising event for the organizations your group supports and that you are excited for them to learn about the groups you are supporting. You do not want anyone thinking that this is a social get-together or networking event, and not about raising money. In any correspondence about the event, be sure to tell people to bring their checkbooks.

Keep the refreshments and décor simple. Some hostesses want to put out a large spread of food, showcase their favorite cocktail, or place decorations throughout their home especially for the event. While the gatherings are meant to be social and fun, their purpose is to focus on the charities we support. Alcohol can change the focus of the event, and too much food will detract from the event's agenda. Overly elaborate refreshments and décor can also intimidate any future hostesses from wanting to open their home, if they feel they would have to provide something similar.

Lining up Your Volunteers

You'll need to have several types of volunteers available to help your gathering run smoothly. With a small gathering, you may need only one of each type. With a larger gathering, you may need two or three people in each role. Here are the types of volunteers we suggest.

Volunteer greeters. It's essential to a successful giving circle that everyone feels welcome as soon as they walk into a gathering. Designate volunteers to welcome everyone as they arrive, thank them for coming, help them sign in, get them a name tag, and introduce them to a couple of people before going back to greeting duties.

These greeters will be in addition to your leadership team members who can also be greeters, but may be busy preparing for the program or making sure the room is set up well. They will need extra support as guests start to arrive.

You might think this is a great job for your more extroverted circle members, but it is also a good job for more introverted members. When introverts have clear tasks and responsibilities, they can also shine, so this is an excellent way to engage shyer members.

Registration volunteers. You'll need volunteers making sure everyone signs in, and collecting contact info, if you don't already have it. These volunteers also help each guest get a name tag, and direct people into the gathering or to a greeter to escort them in. Be sure that your registration volunteers know to be positive and welcoming with everyone. Warmly welcoming each guest is as important as completing the check-in tasks.

Membership and donation volunteers. Make sure you have volunteers who will be responsible for talking to prospective members and collecting donations. Your treasurer or another volunteer will need to speak with any circle members who are behind in their donations to ask that they catch up at this gathering.

Before the program starts, it's a good idea for your volunteers to divide up the list of non-member attendees, assigning each non-member to a volunteer who will see if she has any questions, ask her personally to join the circle, and collect her donation.

Clean-up volunteers. Designate volunteers to stay late and support the hostess in getting her house back in order when your event is in someone's home. This way, the hostess will be happy to host again.

Supplies to Have on Hand

Before the day of the event, you'll also need to prepare the following:

- Handouts about the groups you support
- Audiovisual equipment if you plan to show slides or videos
- Membership/contribution forms
- Extra pens
- RSVP list and name tags for everyone who will be attending
- List of circle members whose donations are in arrears
- Flyers for the next gathering

Planning the Program for Your Gathering

Allow at least thirty minutes for your guests to arrive, get some food and drink, and say hello. Then ask everyone to assemble in one room for the program segment of your gathering. A sample program agenda is included in the Appendix.

Start your program by thanking the hostesses, then share your circle's mission, introduce your leadership team, and have all your guests introduce themselves briefly (in ten seconds or less per person). Ask each person to share if she is a member of the circle. This will inspire guests to join you.

Introductions are an important part of the gathering because women feel more present and relaxed once they have heard their own voice in a room. Also, this is a simple way for everyone to be acknowledged just for attending.

Then acknowledge any new circle members who joined at the last gathering or since. We like to welcome them with a small gift, like a box of tea or a heart-shaped hand mirror. If you have a special name tag for members, this would be a great time to present that to the new folks.

Following this, give an overview of the organizations you support. Share updates from the organizations about what they have accomplished and what your circle has funded since the last gathering. Our charity liaison creates a slideshow for each gathering, which includes PowerPoint slides giving a few basic facts about each organization, plus photos sent by the organization of their recent activities. After giving an overview of each group, she calls on other circle members to read aloud the updates each group has provided.

Next, discuss any group business, like needing hostesses, reminding people to like/follow your giving circle's social media accounts, and sharing the dates to save for your upcoming events.

The final part of the program is the most crucial to your success. Have one of your circle members explain how the circle works, how often you meet, and what the financial pledge and other requirements are to be a member. Then have your treasurer give the financial report of how much has been raised this year, and pass out the forms for today's donations and new members.

While that is happening, have another circle member make the formal ask for contributions and new members. This is when you remind attendees of the purpose for the gathering, and invite them to join your circle. Let guests know that if they cannot join today, their one-time donation is most welcome.

Ask everyone to fill out their membership/contribution forms now. A sample form is provided in the Appendix.

Finally, invite and answer any questions your attendees have. As you conclude your program, tell attendees who to give their membership/contribution form and checks to. Also let guests know that all circle members are available to answer more questions and speak with them individually.

Be sure to involve as many circle members as possible in the program. This will engage your circle members more, and this is also where your future leaders will emerge.

Inviting Guest Presenters from Supported Organizations

After your group has had at least a couple of successful gatherings, consider inviting representatives from your charity partners to present at your gatherings. We suggest that you have only one group's representative at any one gathering. That way, every organization you support can be showcased at a different event. The invited presenter can be the executive director, a program director, or even someone who has been a beneficiary of the organization.

Coach your guest presenter to success by giving them a time limit to present, and asking them to bring photos, video, or PowerPoint slides. Ask them to share specific stories of people or places that have benefited, and how lives have been positively impacted. This will allow your giving circle members to be inspired by the good works their giving is making possible.

Hosting successful gatherings creates a strong and long-lasting giving circle. Follow the ideas presented here to ensure the work is shared and everyone feels welcome, and you will have a meaningful event that raises a substantial amount of money each time.

8: COLLECTING AND DISTRIBUTING DONATIONS

"Shouldn't you put the same amount of effort into your giving as you might for your for-profit investments? After all, philanthropy is an investment, and one in which lives — not profits — are at stake."

**—Laura Arrillaga-Andreessen,
American philanthropist and educator**

Collecting donations for your charities is what your giving circle is all about. While the job of handling donations might not be the most glamorous part of managing a giving circle, it's critically important that it be done well. In this chapter, you'll learn everything you need to know to collect and distribute your circle's donations effectively and consistently.

Collecting Donations from Members and Guests

If you follow the model we're suggesting for forming an independent giving circle, your circle won't have its own bank account, because it will have no legal status as an organization. Even if your circle is affiliated with a specific charity that you're supporting, the circle itself will typically not have a bank account it operates.

If you think you'd rather form a nonprofit to operate your giving circle, you'll need a resource beyond this book to help you. As we explained in the Introduction, you don't need to establish a nonprofit in order to have a thriving circle which makes a significant impact.

With the giving circle model, you'll simply direct your members to make their donations directly to the charity or charities your group supports. Most donations, especially in the beginning, will be given by check at your circle gatherings. (Other methods for collecting donations are described below.) Have your members and their guests write their checks to the charity's name.

Your treasurer will collect these checks, tally them, and mail or deliver them to the appropriate charity. If your giving circle accepts cash, for small amounts, your treasurer can substitute a check of her own to mail. For larger amounts, we recommend she purchase a money order.

We allow our members to split their donation between charities. They can give to two different groups, or donate to all three charities our group supports. Each time a member donates, she can decide what amount to give each one of the three, or she can contribute the full amount of her pledge to just one charity.

When a committed member of your giving circle is unable to attend an event, your treasurer may need to remind the member to send in the pledged amount. The member can either mail a check to your treasurer that is payable to the charity, send her check directly to the charity, or make a donation via the charity's website. If the member chooses to donate to the charity directly, the treasurer should ask the member to forward a copy of her check or receipt, so the Treasurer knows the donation has been made.

Sometimes, your treasurer will need to remind a circle member more than once to make a pledged donation. Don't be hesitant about doing this. Remember: your members have made a commitment to contribute a certain amount in order to join your group. For them to remain members, they must keep their commitment.

As your circle grows and evolves, you may want to encourage members to set up automatic payments to the charities your circle supports. This will reduce your treasurer's workload. Your members can use their bank's bill paying service to have checks or electronic funds transfers (EFTs) sent directly to the charity. For checks, all your members will need is the charity's name and mailing address. For EFTs, members will also need the charity's bank account number and transit/routing number, which the charity can provide you.

Or, your members can set up a recurring donation using their credit card or PayPal. Many charities have an option on their website for making recurring donations. If you don't see this option on a charity's site, just ask them how to accomplish it.

When members are making recurring donations directly to a charity, your treasurer will still need to keep track of these donations. This will enable your circle to accurately measure its impact, and make sure that your members are honoring their pledges. It's best for your treasurer to ask members to provide a copy of their receipts each time a donation is made.

Another approach is to periodically ask the charity for a list of donations made by your members, but not all charities will have the resources to do this for you.

Insight: With Our Donations, They Were Ready When Disaster Struck

In April 2015, a 7.8 magnitude earthquake struck the Kathmandu area of Nepal, killing nearly 9,000 people, and injuring nearly 22,000. We were relieved to hear from our giving circle's Nepali charity partner, TRIFC's Deaf Women's Empowerment Group, that none of the women supported by the project were harmed, and their families were all safe. But the lasting impact of the earthquake was substantial. Over three million people in the area were left homeless, and many lost all their belongings.

One of the items in short supply after the quake was any sort of feminine sanitary protection for the homeless women. The Deaf Women's Empowerment Group had begun exploring how to stitch reusable sanitary protection kits not long before, and they received a request for 1,000 of these kits for earthquake victims!

Because of our giving circle's ongoing contributions, the group had the tools and supplies on hand to fulfill this request: sewing machines, waterproof laminated fabric, and more. With our financial support, the women in the group had already been trained in making these kits, and piloted the kits in their community. Our donations supplied 100% of the funds for this urgent and essential project.

Without our support, the Deaf Women's Empowerment Group would not have been able to help their sisters with this crucial need. But because we had been there to help the women of the group, *they* were there when the women of their community needed them.

Recording and Tracking Donations

To keep accurate records of the donations your circle collects, we recommend that you do the following.

Scan or photograph copies of any checks and contribution forms you receive and upload the images to your group's online file storage area (e.g., Dropbox or Google Drive). That way, they'll be available to any member of your leadership team in case of any questions or discrepancies. Be sure to keep these files private, and only visible to your leadership team members.

Create a spreadsheet showing all donations received, when, from whom, and to which charity they were made. This will enable you to track donations by person, by charity, and by month, quarter, or year. It will also show you which members have not yet honored their pledge for the current period. Keep this spreadsheet in your online file storage area also. (See the Appendix for a sample spreadsheet.)

Have your treasurer report the donation totals for the current period at each meeting of your leadership team, and at each of your events, for everyone to celebrate.

Acknowledging Donations

You'll want to send each member or guest an acknowledgment — by email or postal mail — for the donations she makes to your group's charities. This will allow you to thank her, confirm that her donation has been received, and let her know when to expect an official receipt from the charity. If the member is just joining your circle, your acknowledgment should also welcome her.

The wording of this acknowledgment may be slightly different for the three categories of donors you'll have: new members, continuing members, and event guests. (You'll find examples in the Appendix of the acknowledgments our circle uses.)

Sending Donations to Your Charities

Within a couple of weeks after each event, your treasurer should forward all the donations you've received to your group's charities. Even if you are still waiting for some member pledges to arrive, we recommend you don't delay longer than two weeks to send the contributions you already have. You'll want to enable the charities to deposit the checks promptly to avoid any problems with check-clearing. And, you'll want your members to receive timely receipts from the charities.

Write each charity a cover letter, listing each check enclosed, and giving them the total amount of all checks included. We like to include the donor's email address also, in order to save the charity time and money when sending donor receipts. If your circle's donations are designated for a particular project at the charity, your letter should state that also. (See the Appendix for a sample cover letter.)

What About Charities from Another Country?

Some groups choose to donate to a charity that is not located in their own country and has no sponsor in their country. If you choose to do this, it will require extra work on your treasurer's part, but it can be done. Our circle chose an international charity like this as one of our three beneficiaries. There are three different options you can pursue.

Have your donors contribute cash only. Your treasurer can use the cash to send funds to the charity via international wire transfer. You'll need to let donors know that these contributions will not be tax-deductible, because there is no nonprofit entity involved that is located in your own country. This is a good solution if the amounts donated are relatively small, or you don't plan to donate to this charity for an extended period of time.

Have your treasurer set up a bank account for these donations, and ask donors to make out their checks to this special account. As above, your treasurer can then send the funds via international wire transfer, and the contributions will not be tax-deductible. This is an acceptable interim solution if the amounts donated are small, and you plan to make another arrangement soon. Because the bank account will need to be linked to a tax I.D. number and could trigger federal or local reporting requirements, you don't want to use this method for large amounts or for more than a short period.

As the amounts donated grow and a longer-term relationship with the charity develops, consider finding a charity in your country that will act as the international charity's sponsor, adopting the international charity as one of their funded projects. Then your donors can make their contribution to the sponsoring charity, which in turn will grant the funds to the international charity. This arrangement will make the donations tax-deductible. Ask your members if any of them have relationships with charities that might consider becoming a sponsor.

We were able to make a sponsorship arrangement like this for our circle's international charity, and this sponsorship has had the added benefit of enabling the charity to receive more donations from donors outside our circle as well.

How Well Do Your Recipients Acknowledge You?

As we mentioned in Chapter 3, the best relationships between charities and your giving circle are cultivated when the charity is well aware of your circle's contribution to the charity's success. Ideally, the charity will acknowledge receiving each round of donations, not just to the donors, but also to your treasurer or another representative of your circle.

The charity should also be willing to update your circle at least quarterly on how your funds are being spent. If your circle has a charity liaison, it will be her job to obtain these reports and present them to your members. Regular communication with your charities will allow your leadership team and members to remain confident that your donations are being used well, and that your charities are continuing to operate successfully.

If a charity you have chosen doesn't acknowledge your donations consistently, you may wish to consider switching your support to another charity. Our circle made a change like this at the end of our first year, because one of our three charities wasn't acknowledging our group contributions or updating us on their progress. As a result of making this change, our circle is much more satisfied now with the ongoing relationships we have with the three charities we support.

9: INCLUDING APPRECIATION AND ACKNOWLEDGMENT IN YOUR CIRCLE

"Giving and loving is a beautiful thing. It is the currency of compassion and kindness; it is what separates good people from the rest. And without it, the world would be a bleak place."

—Tiffany Madison, American journalist

Appreciation and gratitude are free, and they are the most valuable tools any group of people have available to build community. Letting the members of your giving circle and leadership team know how much they are appreciated is key to the positive experience and smooth running of your group.

No one can hear "thank you" enough. Everyone loves to be thanked, and when you make it a part of the culture of your group, it will never be forgotten.

Even though the purpose of your group is to serve others, make sure your circle members know they are appreciated by showing them that who they are and what they do matters.

Of course, women will join your circle because they genuinely want to make a difference and help others. Even so, acknowledging their contribution of time and money is still important. Recognize that for some people there is no place in their lives where they are openly appreciated. Plus, everyone will feel good when you take a few moments for appreciation in every gathering, team meeting, or conversation related to your giving circle.

In the powerful book, *The Five Love Languages*, author Gary Chapman shares that not everyone feels love or appreciation the same way. There are actually five different "languages," or ways, for expressing love and appreciation. The book was written for married couples, but the same principles apply to all relationships.

Someone who speaks several different world languages is called a polyglot. We encourage you to be a polyglot of appreciation. Here are the five languages we invite you to become fluent in: Gifts, Quality Time, Words of Appreciation, Acts of Service, and Physical Touch. Let's look at each of these as they apply to appreciation and acknowledgment within your giving circle.

Appreciating with Gifts

Presents are appreciated by most people, even if the item is not exactly what the recipient would like. Many women have gifts as their primary love language. Although your giving circle is most likely self-funded, you probably have members who would be happy to purchase a little something extra to say thank you to others.

At one of our events, each attendee received a box of tea. In that case, one of our members had the tea donated. Another time, we gave heart-shaped tea bag holders to each woman who made a contribution at the event.

When a new member joins our circle, at the next event, we thank her for stepping up by presenting her with a small goodie bag that contains items like fancy chocolates, thank-you cards, or an elegant note pad and pen. We also always have a small gift for each member at our annual member appreciation event that you will read about later in this chapter.

Appreciating with Quality Time

Time to give each other our undivided attention can be created in a variety of ways. For example, members may invite each other to do things together or attend social gatherings together that are unrelated to the giving circle. Everyone values being included. Quality time also consists of taking time to talk to another member when she phones you, or staying late to have a private conversation with someone, and listening more than you talk. One important way that we dedicate quality time in our giving circle is the member appreciation event we hold each year to thank our members.

Words of Appreciation

Giving a verbal acknowledgment of what someone has done makes a person feel seen and heard. "Thank you for coming and supporting our giving circle" would be a *good* verbal acknowledgment. Acknowledgments can also be *excellent* or outstanding.

Instead of just acknowledging someone for what he or she has done, it is far better to acknowledge people for who they are. If you say something like: "You are such a generous person; I so appreciate you always supporting everything I have asked of you over the years," this would be an *excellent* acknowledgment.

An *outstanding* acknowledgment is another level above this. Instead of stopping after acknowledging someone for what they have done and who they are, add a third part. Tell them how that makes you feel or how it has impacted you. You could say: "You were the first person I asked to join our giving circle. I started with you because in ten years of friendship you have never turned down any request I have ever made. You are truly a loyal and supportive friend. Because of your early support, I had the confidence to talk to others. It is because of you that this whole thing got off the ground. Thank you." See how much more impactful that one is?

Acknowledgment is a skill you can build. The more you do it, the better you get, especially if you pursue giving *outstanding* acknowledgments like the one above.

Try to acknowledge people both privately, in one-on-one conversations, and publicly — at your meetings, in your group emails, on your website, or via social media. You could mention them on your group's Facebook page, or from your personal Facebook, Twitter, Pinterest, or Instagram account.

Appreciating with Acts of Service

Doing things for people is a wonderful way of showing appreciation. As you get to know your members, they may make requests of you. They may invite you to a party or workshop they are hosting, or ask you to purchase chocolate bars for their daughter's school fundraiser. When you say yes to these things, that is an act of service. Pay attention to the causes and other fundraising efforts your circle members engage with. Generosity looks good on everyone and it feels good for everyone.

As time passes, your circle membership will become a community. Be sure to let everyone know when a member is taken ill, or a circle member is in need of some extra help or support. If a member is moving or caring for a sick loved one, is there anything other members could do that would help? Even small gestures like dropping off a meal, or sharing a post about a member's fundraiser, will let people know that they are cared for.

Appreciating with Physical Touch

Always be looking for more ways to acknowledge your members. A hello hug is a delightful way to greet people you know, or even people you are meeting for the first time. (Do ask their permission first, if you don't know them well.) This matters because when people feel cared about in your giving circle, they will feel good about being a part of your circle, and that will have them continue as members for a long time.

Insight: Showcase Your Circle Members

To help your circle members feel more engaged, have more fun, and experience more community in your circle, look for ways to showcase their talents.

Barbara McDonald, one of our founding circle members, is also a graphic designer and illustrator. We called on Barbara to design our circle's logo, the template for our email invitations, and flyers for many of our gatherings. At our events, we let everyone know that she has done this for us. Of course we want to thank her for her contribution. We also want to let everyone know what she does for a living, so they may call on her services themselves.

Another of our circle members, Elizabeth Gibbons, is a talented and well-known artist, with a beautiful and unique home. She calls her home the Palace of the Soul, and often rents it out for events. We host some of our events there to showcase her space, and also give her time to announce her upcoming classes and that the space is available to rent. This creates more awareness of her work, and more visibility for her unique space.

When your circle members gain value for their career, business, or family from participating in your circle, they are more likely to remain members, and feel that they are getting a return on their investment of time and money.

Member Appreciation at Gatherings

At each gathering, be sure to acknowledge all your members, and give a special acknowledgment to your new members.

After each gathering, send a thank-you note to all those who made a donation and to those who joined your circle. Even though your circle members pledge to make a regular contribution, it is still important to thank them for their ongoing support.

If you do a post-gathering group email, include a picture of all who attended, naming and thanking them underneath the picture.

If many of your giving circle members use social media, post photos of the gathering, and tag everyone in the pictures. That way you can publicly acknowledge your members, and simultaneously spread the word about your giving circle.

Annual Appreciation of Members

Every year, the Thriving Women in Business Giving Circle hosts a special event just for members that is not about raising funds. Instead, its purpose is to appreciate our members and leadership team. See our agenda for this event in the Appendix. The more your members enjoy being with each other, and value your community, the more they will support your circle and share it with others. Use an event like ours to foster connection and camaraderie among your giving circle members. Do your best to facilitate them socializing and having an enjoyable time.

At our annual member appreciation event, we give a small gift to each member and personally thank and acknowledge each one. One year, our gift was a customized coloring book with images of empowered women and inspirational messages. Another year, we gave every woman a purse hanger to use for hooking her pocketbook underneath the table when dining out.

We ask each member at the event to share what the circle has meant to her during the past year. This is an excellent way to have members affirm the value of their participation, while being publicly acknowledged for it.

Leadership Team Appreciation

With acknowledgment and appreciation as key values for your giving circle, you want to be sure to include it in all your leadership team meetings as well. At every team meeting, thank your team members for their ongoing commitment, and all they do for your giving circle and the causes you support.

At circle gatherings, be sure to introduce your leadership team members and publicly thank them for their work on behalf of the giving circle. Put this on your gathering agenda every time.

Leadership team members are naturally the people who guests will ask questions of, and they will play a hosting role at each event. Consider having a special name badge for them, or a ribbon on their name tags, that identifies them as leadership team members.

Your leadership team's chair may also want to invite the team members for tea or a meal once each year to say thank you and appreciate them again. This will usually become an opportunity to discuss new ideas for your circle. Plus, everyone will have a good time.

Make acknowledgment and appreciation an essential part of your giving circle. You cannot over-acknowledge or over-appreciate people. As long as you are sincere, your members and leadership team will love it.

10: HOW TO MAKE YOUR CIRCLE THRIVE

"We only have what we give."

—Isabel Allende, Chilean-American writer

For the two of us, leading a giving circle has been an incredibly rewarding experience. We're proud of our achievement to have raised $44,000 with our circle in the year before writing this book. The path to our circle's success hasn't always been smooth. We have learned a great deal along the way, and have continued to upgrade how we operate. We want to eliminate some of that learning curve for you. Below are some tips on how to ensure your circle thrives.

Keep Circle Members Engaged

Not every circle member will be involved at the same level. Don't be discouraged if some people don't come to gatherings, or have to be prodded to fulfill their contribution pledges. Be willing to include them at whatever level they choose to participate.

Make sure your charity liaison is updating everyone regularly on the impact your donations are having on the charities you support. Our circle's charity liaison sends an email to each member after every gathering that includes a brief update from each of our supported charities. That way, even members who aren't able to attend all events will feel included.

Help Your Leadership Team Stay Passionate

The more passion your leadership team members have about your circle's mission, the more they will enjoy being part of the team, and the more consistently they will do what they have agreed to. If you have served on any leadership teams, you know that sometimes the organization's activities for members are fun and engaging, while in contrast, serving on the board can sometimes feel frustrating or dull.

One solution for this challenge is to make one of your criteria for leadership team members be that they are passionate about the circle when they start serving. To keep them enthusiastic, try to ensure that no team members are doing too much, and that they get the support they need to do their jobs. Also, check in with your team members occasionally outside meetings to make sure that they are satisfied, and to personally address any concerns or challenges they may have.

It's important to respect that your leadership team members are volunteers, and no doubt have full lives. While you do have to balance that respect with making sure they act responsibly and keep their agreements, you also don't want any team members feeling like they are carrying too much of the work.

Part of what keeps people passionate about what they do is seeing the results of their efforts, which is easy when you share with your team and your members all the valuable work you are doing. Another important part of keeping people enthusiastic is making sure they know their efforts are appreciated. Pay attention to those two things and the level of passion among your team members will stay high.

Plan Gatherings and Meetings Ahead

We encourage you to set your gathering dates as far in advance as possible. This will allow circle members to block out the dates on their calendars, and permit potential members to save the date for the next gathering if they can't make the first one you invite them to. Our circle plans our gathering dates a year in advance, and reminds members and event guests of the upcoming dates regularly.

It's also a good practice to determine your leadership team's meeting dates well ahead of time, so that all team members can arrange to be present. We like to set dates and times for our leadership meetings three months in advance.

Keep Your Circle Visible

Even once you have met your target for the number of circle members you want to have, it's inevitable that some members will drop out or move away from your area. By keeping your circle visible, you'll be in a good position to recruit new members as you need them.

Tell your friends and family members about your circle. If you're active on social media, post photos and updates when your circle has an event. Mention your circle membership in your résumé, professional bio, or social media profiles. Invite guests to your events, whenever appropriate. And ask all your circle members to take these steps as well.

Pay Attention to the Details

Don't fall into the trap of thinking that enthusiasm and desire will make your circle successful without sufficient attention to all the details that will make it so. Tasks that may seem inconsequential — like attending regular leadership team meetings, sending timely reminders to members about upcoming events, or thanking members promptly for contributions — can actually have a significant impact on how members perceive the circle. And that, in turn, will affect your member retention and engagement.

You're taking the trouble to read this book so you can learn about how to start and manage a giving circle. Take the next step, and put into place the systems and structures we've recommended to keep your circle running smoothly.

Ask Your Charities for Specific Results

Your members will truly appreciate it if the charities you support can provide specific details about how your donations are being used. Detailed reports like these will help to keep your members engaged, as well as get prospective members more excited about joining your circle.

For our circle, we ask each of the charities we support to send us a brief update — one page maximum — once per quarter that summarizes what they've accomplished and describes as specifically as they can what our funds have made possible. In an update like this, we might learn that the Deaf Women's Empowerment Group in Nepal purchased a new sewing machine, or that Sakhi for Girls Education has expanded beyond providing books to girls in the slums of Mumbai, and has now added a nutrition program feeding sixty girls two meals per day.

Learning specifics like these enables donors to visualize the impact of their contributions and feel more connected to the charity they are supporting.

Insight: Host a Special Fundraiser

As your giving circle matures, you may wish to find new and different ways for people to connect with your circle. For the Thriving Women in Business Giving Circle, we host an annual one-day fundraising event called Global Love Day. This inspirational day increases awareness of our giving circle and allows us to raise more money for our charity partners. We have found that it is sometimes easier to ask people to get involved for a day, rather than commit to a year of participation.

For Global Love Day, we invite speakers from our community to share their personal stories of overcoming challenges. We host live and silent auctions, serve lunch, and educate guests about the charities we support. When possible, we invite representatives from the charities we support to make presentations about the work they do, and how our giving circle is supporting these efforts. The day is an uplifting experience that allows us to share the work we do in our circle with a wider audience.

To produce an event like this takes a great deal of planning, coordination, and time. You will also need to consult additional resources to make sure you follow any state or local guidelines about public fundraising.

Start well in advance if you want to host a special fundraising event, and be sure to recruit plenty of volunteers who want to get involved. That way, your giving circle's leadership team won't get distracted from the primary mission of your circle and the enrollment of new circle members.

Keep in mind that the more people who know about your giving circle, the more people there will be who choose to support it. An annual fundraiser will increase awareness of your circle, and give people another way to easily support your charity partners. It can be fun, newsworthy, and community-building. Consider adding an event like this to your giving circle's plans as it grows.

Be Loud and Proud about Your Circle's Impact

One of the challenges women sometimes have is that we provide help to others and accomplish important work, but then we stay humble about it. Talking about your giving circle is not the time to be humble. Instead, you want to be loud and proud.

When you share with others the great work your circle is doing, and the impact of your giving, you will get people excited about participating. That is the result you want. It's not the giving that is the exciting part; it's the way you are transforming communities with your giving. Let people know about the amazing things your circle is making possible – via social media, an e-newsletter, or telling people one-on-one. The louder and prouder you and your circle members are, the more successful and sustainable your giving circle will be.

Don't Get Discouraged by Bumps in the Road

There may be times when you feel as if your circle "isn't working." Perhaps it's growing more slowly than you had hoped, or you've recently had several members leave. Or maybe there's been a departure or two from your leadership team, or some team members aren't fulfilling their responsibilities, and others are feeling overloaded.

These are normal occurrences with giving circles, and in fact, with all membership-based, volunteer-run organizations. Don't feel that people leaving or tasks not getting done must mean that you're doing something wrong. You may be doing everything right and still encounter problems with retaining engaged members in your circle and leadership team.

Remind yourself that the current situation is only temporary, and trust that it will turn around if you keep taking steps in the right direction. Has your circle produced *any* donations to the charities you support? Yes? If so, you have made a positive difference in the world already. Focus on the good you are doing, always keeping that in the forefront of your mind as you continue to build your circle.

Share Acknowledgment and Appreciation

One of the best ways to keep members engaged is to acknowledge them often. Follow our suggestions in Chapter 9 on acknowledgment practices you can adopt for your members and your leadership team.

Acknowledgment feels wonderful for both the giver and receiver. True acknowledgment makes people feel seen. With so much time these days spent with electronic devices, acts of acknowledgment by other humans are even more needed because they also make us feel connected. When you incorporate acknowledgment and appreciation as guiding principles for your giving circle (and your life), you will soon learn that they enrich all your relationships.

Facilitate Community Among Members

Belonging is a basic human need. For most women, it is essential to our happiness. The best part of your giving circle, beyond the significant impact you can have, will be the women you will meet and get to know. When your members gather with your circle of like-hearted, like-minded women, they will make friends, cultivate connections that lead to other activities together, and enrich each other's lives in numerous ways.

Be sure to encourage your members to socialize with each other at your gatherings, and to get together at other times. For example, we are always happy when our members network with each other to build their businesses, as long as this is done graciously. The more you can foster special relationships among your members, the better.

In Chapter 9, we described our annual appreciation event for circle members. We've found this event to be important for fostering community. Facilitating community is part of what will keep your members coming back.

Have Fun with Your Circle

Between the two of us, we have attended thousands of events. Most of them, we have completely forgotten. Why? Because they were not memorable.

Fun makes an event memorable. Look for ways to add fun to your gatherings. Perhaps you can designate a theme for your gathering. This could be a seasonal theme, like love in February, or a topical theme, such as women at work.

At one of our circle's summer gatherings the host chose a Hawaiian luau theme, including a life-size cutout of Elvis in swim trunks for attendees to pose with for pictures. For another event, a volunteer decorated cupcakes to look like tiny tea tables, complete with cups and saucers molded from fondant.

Fun can also be added with a brief presentation on a related topic. Once when we hosted our gathering at a local tea parlor, we had a speaker give a five-minute presentation on the history of tea. For another gathering, we asked a woman in our community who is a magician to perform. In just a few minutes, she presented an illusion that showed how we are all connected. These brief sessions were captivating and memorable. Taking a few minutes to include some fun in your gathering's agenda is always a rewarding idea.

Experiencing an event as fun also comes from feeling like you're part of what's going on. When you are seen and acknowledged, you feel welcome and included. We have all walked into a room where no one came to greet us, or where everyone but us seemed to know someone. In our circle, we put a lot of attention on making sure everyone feels welcome, appreciated, and included. Make that an intention in your circle as well.

When everyone feels included, everything that happens is more enjoyable. When your circle members always feel like they are a significant part of the great work you are doing, they will want to remain in your circle for a long time to come.

APPENDIX

Appendix Contents

Giving Circle Start-Up Checklist

☐ Get clear on your commitment (Chapter 1)

☐ Assemble your organizing team (Chapter 1)

☐ Establish your circle's mission (Chapter 2)

☐ Name your circle (Chapter 2)

☐ Create criteria for choosing organizations to support (Chapter 3) [skip this and the other Chapter 3 steps if your circle is already affiliated with a charity]

☐ Search for and research appropriate charities (Chapter 3)

☐ Contact potential charity partners (Chapter 3)

☐ Choose which organizations your circle will initially support (Chapter 3)

☐ Design criteria for selecting your leadership team (Chapter 4)

☐ Develop job descriptions for your leadership team (Chapter 4)

☐ Enroll leadership team members (Chapter 4)

☐ Schedule planning meetings with your leadership team (Chapter 5)

☐ Decide who your circle members will be (Chapter 6)

☐ Determine how much each circle member will contribute (Chapter 6)

☐ Plan when and where your first circle gathering will take place (Chapter 6)

☐ Write a description of your group to share with prospective members (Chapter 6)

☐ Identify and invite potential members to your first gathering (Chapter 6)

☐ Plan the refreshments and décor for your gathering (Chapter 7)

☐ Prepare materials and supplies for your gathering (Chapter 7)

☐ Line up volunteers to assist with your gathering (Chapter 7)

☐ Design the program for your gathering (Chapter 7)

☐ Hold your first circle gathering (Chapter 7)

☐ Welcome new circle members and acknowledge their donations (Chapters 6 and 8)

☐ Record and distribute collected donations to your charity partners (Chapter 8)

☐ Acknowledge your leadership team and volunteers for a job well done (Chapter 9)

☐ Begin planning your next gathering (Chapters 7 and 10)

Sample Leadership Team Job Descriptions

Duties of all leadership team members:

- Keep confidential all information shared in team meetings, and learned about circle members.
- Speak only positively about our circle and other team and circle members.
- Remain in good standing as a circle member, making all pledged contributions on time.
- Attend all circle gatherings (one absence allowed per year).
- Arrive one hour early for all quarterly gatherings to help set up.
- Attend all virtual team meetings (occasional absence is okay).
- Host or co-host a circle gathering once per year.
- Be loud and proud about our circle, inviting many people to join us.
- Plan to bring two to four guests to each quarterly gathering.
- Respond to team communications within one business day.
- If you find you're not able to perform one of your duties, let us know so someone else can handle it.
- Serve on the leadership team for at least one year from your start date.

Circle chair:

- Put together leadership team meeting agenda.
- Facilitate leadership team meetings.
- Create the agenda for each quarterly gathering.
- Create the agenda for the annual circle member appreciation event.
- Host or co-host the annual circle member appreciation event.

- Follow up with team members to make sure all tasks assigned to them are completed.

Treasurer:

- Bring membership/contribution forms to each gathering.
- Collect forms and checks/cash from donors at quarterly gatherings and by mail.
- Provide information about new members to PR chair, secretary, and membership chair.
- Scan all checks and forms received; upload to Dropbox.
- Send email acknowledgment to each donor.
- Send automatic payment instructions to new members.
- For small cash donations, deposit into own bank account and write own check to charities. For large donations, use cash to purchase a money order.
- Send donation checks and cover letters to charities promptly.
- Maintain a spreadsheet recording all donations each quarter, also showing outstanding pledges.
- Inform leadership team monthly of total donations received for the quarter, subtotaled by charity.
- Answer questions from members and guests about donating.
- Follow up with circle members who don't attend quarterly gatherings to secure their donations.
- Report to leadership team quarterly on total donations per charity received, year to date and all time.

Secretary:

- Send out leadership team meeting reminder two days before each meeting.
- Take team meeting minutes, post to Dropbox, and send to team members.

- Keep track of important action items and remind other team members of due dates when needed.

- Maintain roster of circle members and leadership team members with complete contact information.

- Add all new members to Constant Contact mailing list.

- Produce event roster for each gathering and mark on roster all who attended.

- Maintain list of prospective circle members and gathering attendees in Constant Contact.

- Transfer new names from Eventbrite RSVPs to Constant Contact mailing list after each gathering.

- Maintain list of past and future gatherings, including dates, locations, and hosts/co-hosts.

- Send leadership team a list of who has RSVP'd three weeks, two weeks, and one week before each gathering.

- Send out thank-you cards to all attendees (members and guests) after each gathering.

- Send "save the date" email with all gatherings for the next year to circle members after each gathering.

- Maintain schedule of when pre-gathering and post-gathering email announcements should be sent.

- Respond to emails/voice mails for our circle, or forward to appropriate leadership team member.

Charity liaison:

- Identify new potential charity partners for our circle's mission when needed.

- Perform a due diligence review on any new potential charities.

- Initiate member vote on charity partners each November.

- Obtain updates from each charity partner before each gathering.

- Organize charity partner reports for presentation at gatherings.

- Present charity partner reports at gatherings or recruit other members to do so.

- Circulate charity partner reports to all circle members after each gathering.

- Serve as liaison between our circle and charity partners for any needs/questions

Membership chair:

- Welcome and thank all circle members for attending at each gathering.

- Phone each new member to welcome and arrange for hosting/co-hosting a gathering.

- Arrange for a gift for each new member at the next gathering.

- Invite and cultivate non-members at each gathering to join our circle.

- Arrange for hosts and co-hosts for each quarterly gathering.

- Provide information from hosts to PR/marketing chair for updating Eventbrite RSVP page and web page with new date, time, location, and event-specific info for each gathering.

- Call non-member attendees after the gathering, thank them for coming, tell them when the next gathering is, and ask if they have any interest in joining our circle.

- Maintain a list of past attendees who may become members, and past registrants who didn't attend, and follow up appropriately.

- Call all circle members two weeks before each gathering to make sure they are coming and remind them to invite guests.

PR/marketing chair:

- Create flyer for each gathering, share with leadership team, and bring copies to prior gathering.

- Create social media image for each gathering and share with leadership team and members.

- Set up Eventbrite RSVP page, confirmation, and reminder email for each gathering.

- Email announcements/invitations to Constant Contact mailing list three times per quarter: one week after gathering, one month before gathering, and one week before gathering.

- Create and bring guest name tags for all non-member attendees to each gathering.

- Create a special member nametag for each new member.

- Take photos or recruit others to do so at each gathering, upload to Dropbox, and post to Facebook.

- Follow up with new members to add their information to member section of circle web page.

- Update circle web page each quarter with date and location of next gathering.

- Post an update to the circle Facebook page at least once per week, and respond to comments/messages from visitors on a timely basis.

Member at large:

- Hold a focus on attracting new prospective members to our gatherings.

- Assist with other leadership team responsibilities as needed.

Sample Group Description
and Membership Requirements

The Thriving Women in Business Giving Circle gathers women together to uplift the lives of women and girls around the world. We are a women's giving circle. Our circle hosts quarterly gatherings to raise money for education and entrepreneurship training for developing world women and girls. We select three charities to support each year. We are advocates for all women being philanthropists and community stewards, regardless of their wealth.

Membership requirements: The Thriving Women in Business Giving Circle requests that our members pledge to donate each year $1,000 or more in total contributions to the three charities we support. You may choose how much of your donation goes to each charity.

Contributions can be made monthly, quarterly, or annually. Members are invited to our quarterly giving circle gatherings, and encouraged to bring guests. Attendance at giving circle events is not required for membership.

Sample Personal Invitation

Subject: Inviting you to learn about our giving circle

[First Name], I thought you might be interested in being part of our giving circle of Bay Area women who support the education and economic empowerment of women and girls in the developing world.

I've been on the leadership team of the Thriving Women in Business Giving Circle since 2015. We meet together four times per year to pool our donated funds to support charitable projects that carry out our mission. The recipients report back to us on how our donations are spent, and we share these reports at each gathering, along with videos, photos, or guest speakers.

It's a rewarding and fun way to contribute to the advancement of developing world women and girls. You get to participate in the decision of how your donations are used, develop relationships with the other members of the circle and the recipients of the circle's funds, and have more impact and connection than is possible when you make charitable donations independently. Plus, you get to spend a rewarding afternoon with a great group of women!

We are hosting our next meeting on Sunday, April 30, from 1-3 p.m. in San Francisco. You would be welcome to attend as a prospective member or as a guest. There is no charge to attend; we simply ask that you make a contribution of any amount you choose. 100% of your donation goes to charity, and is tax-deductible.

The idea behind our giving circle is simple. Women love to get together, converse, share ideas, do good, and have fun. Sometimes modern life does not offer enough opportunity for these pleasures. Participating in our circle allows women to do what they love, while uplifting the lives of women and girls around the world. What could be better?

Would you like to join us at our April gathering?

Warmly,
[First Name]

Sample Email Announcement to Mailing List

Subject: Let's Change the World Together

Have you been meaning to join us? Every quarter, the Thriving Women in Business Giving Circle gathers together awesome women like you to hear inspirational stories about the women and girls we support.

In a single afternoon, we funded the manufacture of over 200 reusable sanitary protection kits by the Deaf Women's Empowerment Group for earthquake victims in Nepal. In a single afternoon, we provided 300 girls in the slums of Mumbai with weekly books delivered to their door by Sakhi for Girls' Education. And in a single afternoon, we helped ten women caring for AIDS orphans in Zambia to launch businesses which will enable them to feed their families and obtain necessary health care.

You are invited to be part of our work to uplift women and girls in the developing world, and be uplifted yourself in return. 100% of the funds we raise goes directly to our charity partners.

Join us in the Montclair district of Oakland on July 31st from 2-4 p.m. for an afternoon of refreshments, inspiration, and good deeds. The address and other details will be given with your RSVP. Click here to reserve your place.

Your friends at the Thriving Women in Business Giving Circle

Sample Event Flyer

Join us to uplift the lives of women and girls in one afternoon!

You're invited to meet our ongoing giving circle of San Francisco Bay Area women, who gather quarterly and pool our funds to support women and girls in the developing world. Learn more about our circle at twibc.com/givingcircle

Sunday, January 29, 2017

2:00-4:00 p.m.

Tal y Tara Tea & Polo Shoppe

6439 California St, San Francisco

RSVP at twibgc.eventbrite.com

Questions? Contact:

Caterina Rando, cat@caterinarando.com, (415) 668-4535

C.J. Hayden, cjh@cjhayden.com, (415) 981-8845

Sample Membership/Contribution Form

THRIVING WOMEN IN BUSINESS GIVING CIRCLE
MEMBERSHIP/CONTRIBUTION FORM

Name: _____

Email Address: _____

Best Phone Number: _____

Mailing Address: _____

_____

☐ I'm ready to become a member of the Thriving Women in Business Giving Circle. I commit to contributing $1000 or more each year (only $83.33 per month) and to host or co-host a gathering every other year.

☐ I'm already a member of the Thriving Women in Business Giving Circle.

☐ I'm not ready to become a Giving Circle member today, but I would like to stay informed about Thriving Women in Business. Please keep me on your contact list.

☐ I am donating today to one or more of the charities supported by the circle. (Giving Circle members should give a total of $250 or more. Non-members may give any amount.)

   ☐ Deaf Women's Empowerment Group
     (check payee: TRIFC)   _____

   ☐ Sakhi for Girls' Education
     (check payee: Citizen Angel)   _____

   ☐ Zambian Women Entrepreneurs
     (check payee: Power of Love)   _____

                  Total   _____

(continued on next page)

To pay for my donation:

☐ I'm enclosing _____ in cash.

☐ I'm enclosing check(s) payable to TRIFC, Citizen Angel, and/or Power of Love.

(All donations are tax-deductible as charitable contributions to the extent allowed by law. You will receive an email receipt.)

Thank you for supporting women and girls in the developing world!

Forgot your checkbook? Mail checks to: Caterina Rando, P.O. Box XXXX, San Francisco, CA 94121

Thriving Women in Business Giving Circle
givingcircle@twibc.com · 415-851-GIVE (4483)
twibc.com/givingcircle

Sample Giving Circle Hostess Guide

HOW TO BE A GREAT HOSTESS
FOR GIVING CIRCLE GATHERINGS

Thank you for hosting a gathering for the Thriving Women in Business Giving Circle. This will be easy and fun to do. Here's a step-by-step guide to hosting a successful event.

BEFORE YOUR EVENT

1. Give our membership chair any details guests will need. These might include instructions for finding your home, where to park, or if there are any pets in the home a guest might be allergic to.

2. Contact your co-hosts. Every time we have an event we have co-hosts to support the "anchor hostess." The anchor hostess is usually the woman who is opening her home to the event, but sometimes will be a designated leadership team member. Schedule a time to speak with your co-hosts and discuss who is responsible for what.

3. Put together your invitation list. Even though we will invite our TWIBGC mailing list and our giving circle members will invite their friends, we find the hostess is well positioned to bring new women to our events.

Invite your best friends, relatives, business colleagues, neighbors, and women you haven't seen in a long time. This is a great time to reconnect! Also, invite women you do not know very well and would like to get to know better. Invite any woman you think would be a good match for what we are up to with our giving circle. We ask that guests leave children at home unless they are girls 12 years of age and over.

4. Invite more than you think. People's lives are busy and full. Not everyone will be able to attend. Inviting 50-60 people is not too many. We often have a no-show rate of 30% or more.

5. Know the numbers. We are looking for an RSVP list of 40 or more. That usually means we will have around 30 in attendance. Be sure that your guests RSVP so we have an accurate count of RSVPs. If someone tells you she is coming, but you don't see her on the RSVP list, add her to the list yourself.

6. Get in touch personally. We find that emails are often not read and that a personal invitation to attend goes far to fill the room. Call or send a personal message via social media or text (however your friends typically communicate) to let people know you want them to attend.

7. Ask for a donation. If someone cannot attend, ask her to make a donation to one of our three charities and send it to you before your event. This way you can count her donation toward total donations resulting from the event. *Be sure to tell her to make out the check directly to the charity.*

8. Confirm all guests the day before. Without a confirmation reminder to your guests saying you are looking forward to seeing them at the event, you can have a drop-off rate of up to 50% from your yes RSVPs.

PLANNING YOUR EVENT

1. Do not plan a huge spread. This will intimidate your guests from hosting their own gathering. We want everyone to see how easy it is to host. We want you to enjoy the event. If you are in and out of the kitchen throughout your whole event, the guests will miss you and you will not have as much fun.

2. Skip the alcohol. Our events are alcohol-free. We promise your guests will all leave feeling great because of the giving.

3. Ask someone else to care for your pets and children. We ask that pets and children not be present during our events.

4. Coordinate audio/visual needs with our charity liaison. We like to show photos, slides, and sometimes videos at our events. Plan ahead where this can take place in your home, and speak with our charity liaison about what equipment you have vs. what others will need to bring.

DURING YOUR EVENT

1. Ask co-hosts to help. Your co-hosts are there to support you; don't hesitate to ask them to pitch in when something needs attention.

2. Introduce guests to one another. We want everyone to feel welcome at our events. Facilitate people meeting each other and have your eyes open for the person who may not know anyone.

3. Have a good time! Remember, you're among friends, many of whom you may not have seen in a while, so enjoy your time with them. Be 100% set up before your guests arrive, so you can enjoy them.

That's all there is to it! We promise you that you will feel great afterwards. We always do. It's such a fun and powerful way to help change and uplift the lives of women and girls.

We thank you for your kind and generous heart in supporting women and girls around the world.

Sample Program Agenda for Gatherings

PROGRAM AGENDA: JULY 2017 GATHERING

12:00 p.m. Leadership team arrives

1:00 p.m. Arrival of guests: Leadership team and greeters welcome members and guests

1:30 p.m. Program begins:

- Circle chair — Thank the hostess and co-hosts for today; introduce leadership team members.

- PR/marketing chair — Invite attendees to introduce themselves, say if they are members of the giving circle, and if so, to share why (briefly).

- Circle chair — Share how we got started and our mission:

  The Thriving Women in Business Giving Circle gathers women together to support better lives for women and girls around the world. We are a giving circle — a group who joins together to support the causes of our choice. Our circle pools our funds to donate to specific causes and hosts gatherings to increase members' awareness about the causes we support. We decide together where our funds should go.

- Charity liaison — Describe our three charity partners and present their quarterly reports.

- Secretary — Explain how the circle works, e.g., members pledge to donate $1,000 over the course of a year to our charity partners; the circle hosts quarterly gatherings.

- Membership chair — Make the ask for donations; invite all guests to become members today.

- Circle chair — Briefly reiterate the ask and see if any questions.

- Treasurer — Pass out contribution/membership forms, collect forms and donations.

- Membership chair — Ask people to fill out their forms and turn them in now so we can celebrate them; take a pause for people to do that. Acknowledge any new members.

- PR/marketing chair — Share the date of our next gathering. Thank everyone for coming and request again that they join us and spread the word of what we are up to.

3:00 p.m. Program concludes

Sample Donation Tracking Spreadsheet

Name	Auto Pay?	Charity 1	Charity 2	Charity 3	Owes
Member 1	N/A	75.00	100.00	75.00	0
Member 2	N/A	150.00	0	0	100
Member 3	N/A	333.00	333.00	334.00	0
Member 4	Monthly	28	28	28	168
Member 5	N/A	0	0	0	250
Guest 1	N/A	0	0	100	0
Total		586	461	237	518

Total Collected 1st Quarter	1802
Total Collected YTD	1802

Notes:

Our circle collects pledged donations on a quarterly basis, so that's how the above spreadsheet is organized. If your circle will collect pledged donations monthly or annually instead of quarterly, you'll need to adjust the format to match your structure.

The example above assumes it's the first quarter of the year, and members are pledging $1000 per year or $250 per quarter. At the end of the first month, here's where the six people listed above stand:

- Member 1 — First quarter pledge paid in full; owes nothing until second quarter

- Member 2 — Paid $150 of 1st quarter pledge; still owes $100 for first quarter. Treasurer must follow up.

- Member 3 — Paid full year pledge of $1000; owes nothing until next year.

- Member 4 — Making automatic payments monthly; still owes two more months of payments for first quarter. No

need for Treasurer to follow up, as payments will be
processed later in quarter.

- Member 5 — Has made no payments this quarter. Treasurer
  must follow up.

- Guest 1 — Made a one-time contribution of $100. No need
  for Treasurer to follow up, but Membership Chair may wish
  to pursue this person as a member.

For each pledge period — each quarter, in our example — you'll
want to add four more columns to your spreadsheet to track the
payments to each charity for the new period, plus any amounts still
owed. At the end of the year, you'll start a new spreadsheet and
begin tracking the new year's pledges.

Sample Contribution/Membership Acknowledgment for New Members

Subject: Welcome to the TWIB Giving Circle

Dear [Member First Name]:

Thank you for becoming a member of the Thriving Women in Business Giving Circle! You have joined a giving circle of women who meet quarterly and each pledge to give $1,000 annually to support the education and economic empowerment of women and girls in the developing world. We support projects that further women's entrepreneurship and girls' education.

We appreciate your donation of $[Amount] to [Charity 1] and $[Amount] to [Charity 2]. Your generosity will go far and has the potential to affect many generations of women and their children to come.

We will hold your funds for a short time while we collect pledges from those unable to attend the gathering. Then your funds will be sent directly to the charities you selected. You should be receiving receipts from the organizations within two months of the gathering. If you do not receive a receipt, please email me and I will research this for you. All your donations are tax-deductible as charitable contributions to the extent allowed by law.

You are welcome to make your contribution(s) by check each quarter, however, many of our members find it more convenient to make contributions monthly. Attached are instructions for how to set up automatic payments with each charity by credit card or your bank's bill paying service.

We would love to list you as a member on our web page at www.twibc.com/givingcircle. Just reply to this email and let me know if you have a site or page you'd like your name to link to.

Please take a moment to like the TWIB Giving Circle page on Facebook at www.facebook.com/TWIBGivingCircle/ and consider inviting your friends to like the page also.

We look forward to seeing you at our next gathering on [Date] at [Location] in [City] and getting to know you better. We invite you to bring a friend who shares your support for developing world women and girls.

Thanks again for your contribution!

Warmly,

Thriving Women in Business Giving Circle Leadership Team:

Caterina Rando
C.J. Hayden
Barbara McDonald
Anna Marks
Stephie Zuendorf
Judy Foley
Hema Ganapathy

www.twibc.com/givingcircle

Sample Contribution Acknowledgment
for Continuing Members

Subject: Thank you for your TWIBGC contribution

Dear [Member First Name]:

Thank you for continuing your membership in the Thriving Women in Business Giving Circle and attending our last gathering! We appreciate your donation of $[Amount] to [Charity 1] and $[Amount] to [Charity 2]. The women and girls supported by your donations appreciate your generosity.

We will hold your funds for a short time while we gather up pledges from those unable to attend the gathering. Then your funds will be sent directly to the charities you selected. You should be receiving receipts from the organizations within two months of the gathering. If you do not receive a receipt, please email me and I will research this for you. All donations are tax-deductible as charitable contributions to the extent allowed by law.

We look forward to seeing you at our next gathering on [Date] at [Location] in [City]. We invite you to bring a friend who shares your support for developing world women and girls.

Thanks again for your contribution!

Warmly,

Thriving Women in Business Giving Circle Leadership Team:

Caterina Rando
C.J. Hayden
Barbara McDonald
Anna Marks
Judy Foley
Stephie Zuendorf
Hema Ganapathy

www.twibc.com/givingcircle/

Sample Contribution Acknowledgment
for Non-Member Attendees

Subject: Thank you for your TWIBGC contribution

Dear [Guest First Name]:

Thank you for attending our last gathering of the Thriving Women in Business Giving Circle! We appreciate your donation of $[Amount] to [Charity 1]. You are supporting the education and economic empowerment of women and girls in the developing world. Your generosity will go far and has the potential to affect many generations of women and their children to come.

We will hold your funds for a short time while we gather up pledges from those unable to attend the gathering. Then your funds will be sent directly to the charities you selected. You should be receiving receipts from the organizations within two months of the gathering. If you do not receive a receipt, please email me and I will research this for you. All donations are tax-deductible as charitable contributions to the extent allowed by law.

We'll keep you up to date on our activities and we hope one day you'll become a member. We hope to see you at our next gathering on [Date] at [Location] in [City]. We invite you to bring a friend who shares your support for developing world women and girls.

Thanks again for your contribution!

Warmly,

Thriving Women in Business Giving Circle Leadership Team:

Caterina Rando
C.J. Hayden
Barbara McDonald
Anna Marks
Judy Foley
Stephie Zuendorf
Hema Ganapathy

www.twibc.com/givingcircle/

Sample Donation Cover Letter to Charities

[Charity Contact Name]

[Charity Name]

[Charity Address]

Dear [Charity Contact First Name],

Enclosed you will find checks totaling $[Amount] from Thriving Women in Business Giving Circle members and guests at our [Event Date] event. Please make sure these donors receive receipts for their contributions. The donors are as follows:

[Donor 1 Name]   [Donor 1 Email]   [Donor 1 Donation Amount]

[Donor 2 Name]   [Donor 2 Email]   [Donor 2 Donation Amount]

[Donor 3 Name]   [Donor 3 Email]   [Donor 3 Donation Amount]

These donations are for the benefit of [Charity Name]'s [Program Name].

Warmly,

Thriving Women in Business Giving Circle Leadership Team:

Caterina Rando
C.J. Hayden
Barbara McDonald
Anna Marks
Judy Foley
Stephie Zuendorf
Hema Ganapathy

www.twibc.com/givingcircle

Sample Program Agenda
for Annual Member Appreciation Event

12:00 p.m. Leadership team arrives

1:00 p.m. Arrival of members; welcomed by leadership team

1:30 p.m. Program begins:

- Circle chair — Thank host; introduce leadership team members; thank them for their service.

- Membership chair — Acknowledge any new circle members; thank everyone for coming: "Because of you we are able to uplift women and girls."

- PR/marketing chair — Invite circle members to introduce themselves (briefly).

- Charity liaison — Overview of what our work has done this past year; share year-end messages from our charity partners.

- Secretary — Ask for confirming vote on supporting same three charities for the next twelve months.

- Treasurer — Financial report of what we have raised this year for each organization.

- Membership chair — remind everyone of the next gathering date and location; ask for hostesses for upcoming gatherings; remind everyone to invite new prospective members.

- PR/marketing chair — Remind everyone to promote our gatherings online; like, share and comment about circle activities; like our Facebook page.

- Circle chair — Vision for this past year was thirty members, we are currently at twenty-nine. Next year we would like to expand to forty members.

- Membership chair — Pass out gathering flyers for next year; go over the dates and any gatherings we still need co-hosts for.

- Circle chair — Thank members for coming; encourage them to stay and visit, enjoy food and beverages, participate in bonding activity (e.g., art project, year-end ritual).

3:00 p.m. Program concludes

Recommended Resources

Canada Revenue Agency Charities Listings — For Canadians, these listings provide insight into a charity's program activities and finances. (The U.S. equivalent is Guidestar, below.)

www.cra-arc.gc.ca/chrts-gvng/lstngs/

Forum of Regional Associations of Grantmakers — You can learn more about the impact of giving circles and best practices for operating one from this organization.

www.givingforum.org/topic/giving-circles

"Getting Together to Give" — This article in the Stanford Social Innovation Review by Laura Arrillaga-Andreessen is what first got the authors excited about the potential of giving circles.

www.ssir.org/articles/entry/giving_2.0_getting_together_to_give

Giving 2.0, **Laura Arrillaga-Andreessen** — Laura's book provides many helpful tips for identifying your mission and vetting potential charity partners.

www.laaf.org/the-book/

Giving Circles Fund — Provides resources to giving circle founders and members, including guides to help you choose your mission, vet charity partners, and facilitate your circle.

www.givingcirclesfund.org/learn/

Guidestar — For the U.S., these listings provide insight into a charity's program activities and finances. (The Canadian equivalent is Canada Revenue Agency, above.)

www.guidestar.org

Wikipedia Giving Circle Entry — Wikipedia offers a collection of examples of existing giving circles, as well as providing additional giving circle resources.

en.wikipedia.org/wiki/Giving_circle

Connect with Our Giving Circle

We've provided you with a wealth of information in this book that will support you in building a thriving giving circle. We also know that many of us learn best by watching others doing what we want to do. If you live in the San Francisco Bay Area, or plan to visit, we graciously invite you to join us at one of our quarterly giving circle gatherings.

Come early, stay late, ask questions, and let us show you how we operate. Take away what you like, and notice what you will want to do differently. We would welcome the opportunity to model for you how a successful circle works, and to inspire you in person.

On our circle's web page, you will find information on our upcoming gatherings, our circle members, and the organizations we are currently supporting. Please join our mailing list for the latest news about us and invitations to our events.

Visit our web page at www.twibc.com/givingcircle/

Like our Facebook page at

www.facebook.com/TWIBGivingCircle

Support Our Charity Partners

We are honored to support three organizations that do incredible work in their communities to uplift the lives of women and girls through entrepreneurship training and education. Watching these organizations, and the people they serve, thrive because of our contributions is our greatest gift from our giving circle. If you would like to help them also, please reach out to them, and let them know how you heard about their work.

Power of Love Foundation — www.poweroflove.org

Program: Women Entrepreneurs Program — Provides business training, mentoring, and microloans to unemployed women caring for multiple children in AIDS-stricken communities.

Location: Matero, Lusaka, Zambia

Directed by: Alka Subramanian, San Diego, CA

Sakhi for Girls Education — www.sakhiforgirlseducation.org

Program: Girls Learning Centre — Serves girls living in slums, offering a safe place to gather, providing books and cultural experiences, teaching literacy, and building life skills.

Location: Mulund, Mumbai, India

Directed by: Aarti Naik, Mumbai, India

The Rose International Fund for Children — www.trifc.org

Program: Deaf Women's Empowerment Group — Gives deaf women skills to become productive members of their households and society, provides them with community, shows value of the differently abled.

Location: Banepa, Nepal

Directed by: Rob Rose, TRIFC Director, and Rose Stevens, DWEG Coordinator, Bellevue, WA

ABOUT THE AUTHORS

C.J. Hayden

C.J. has spent much of the last twenty-five years supporting women and girls in becoming economically self-sufficient. She believes in the possibility of business as a force for good, and that empowering women and girls throughout the world would solve many of our planet's problems.

Since 1992, C.J. has been a business coach to self-employed professionals and small business owners, including many who think of themselves as social entrepreneurs. Her coaching and training clients have included Ashoka Youth Venture, Grameen Shakti, Green America, Leaderspring, and National Indian Justice Center.

C.J. holds the credentials Master Certified Coach and Certified Professional Co-Active Coach, and is a member of the Arbinger Coaching Network. She was an early leader in the growing coaching profession, serving on the founding board of the Professional and Personal Coaches Association (later merged with the International Coach Federation).

Throughout her career, C.J. has served pro bono on boards and committees for numerous organizations, including Women's Economic Network, Women in Business Mentoring Circles, San Francisco Business & Professional Women, and the San Francisco chapter of the Social Enterprise Alliance. She is currently the director of the charitable nonprofit Citizen Angel and co-founder of the giving circle A3: Access, Advancement, Autonomy.

C.J. is the author of four books, including the bestseller *Get Clients Now!* and *50 Ways Coaches Can Change the World*. She has taught for Mills College and John F. Kennedy University. C.J. speaks and writes for international audiences on business-building, writing, and changemaking. Find out more about C.J. at www.cjhayden.com.

Caterina Rando

Caterina is the Italian-American granddaughter of Ellis Island immigrants. She grew up in a household where she was taught to be grateful for what she had, while being aware that many had much less. She has been a philanthropist and a facilitator of giving since she raised money in grammar school for missionaries. In high school, she organized the school's first annual blood drive and began to see the power of gathering women together for good.

The philanthropic project Caterina is most proud of is enrolling 100 people in donating funds to purchase a bench in San Francisco's Golden Gate Park for Irv Spivak, a man usually very positive, who was uncharacteristically depressed for too long. This act of giving skyrocketed his spirits and made such a difference that gratitude, community, and joy flourished in him for the rest of his life.

Caterina is also a graduate of Leadership San Francisco, a community stewardship program that supports and develops community leaders. Over her career, Caterina has served on the boards of multiple organizations, including The Women's Foundation, San Francisco Business and Professional Women, and The San Francisco Chamber of Commerce.

Caterina has been serving women entrepreneurs on a mission for over twenty-five years. She achieved the designation of Master Certified Coach, and is the author of *Learn to Think Differently* and co-author of *The ABCs of Public Speaking, Woman Entrepreneur Extraordinaire*, and *Savvy Leadership Strategies for Women*.

A sought-after speaker, Caterina has served audiences around the globe and produces over seventy-five days of women's events each year, including group training programs, business development summits, and personal retreats. She is an advocate for being authentic and purposeful in your business, while being profitable and contributing to your community. Find out more about Caterina at www.caterinarando.com.

Invite Us to Speak or Train for You

We are passionate about spreading the word regarding the power and ease of using giving circles to uplift communities and causes. The two of us have been speaking and providing trainings to audiences both large and small for many years. We have seen how one idea in one speech or workshop can ignite a spark that creates a flame to fuel a person, a project, or even a movement.

We would welcome a discussion with you to explore whether we could present to your group, conference, or event. The feedback from your participants will be enthusiastic and positive, as it has been with the hundreds of audiences we have served.

Here are topics we present on regularly:

- How to Start a Giving Circle and Change the World
- How to Energize Your Charitable Cause for Growth
- Spend Your Social Capital to Maximize Impact

Please contact us by email or through either of our websites:

C.J. Hayden	**Caterina Rando**
contact@cjhayden.com	**cat@caterinarando.com**
www.cjhayden.com	**www.caterinarando.com**

ACKNOWLEDGMENTS

Caterina Rando: I will always be grateful to my mom and dad, Anthony and Maria Gloria Rando, who have modeled generosity and giving my whole life. They showed me that being of service feels great and that there is plenty to go around.

C.J. Hayden: Heartfelt thanks to my life partner "Friendly Dave" Herninko, who kept me fueled with hot meals and warm hugs throughout the writing of this book, and to my fellow members of Shut Up & Write for keeping my fingers on the keyboard.

We both wish to acknowledge the following people whose contributions made this book possible.

The generous members of the Thriving Women in Business Giving Circle, A Good Deed Tea, and A³: Access - Advancement - Autonomy, who have supported our work and enriched our lives.

The hard-working leaders of the charities our giving circle supports: Aarti Naik, Alka Subramanian, Robert Rose, and Rose Stevens. Your example inspires us every day.

Our beta readers Tracy Creer, Judy Foley, Laura Gisborne, Kariz Matic, Paula Pacheco, and Susan Urquhart-Brown.

Our friends and colleagues Maggie Oman Shannon and Valerie Camarda, whose early encouragement launched us on the giving circle path.

www.ingramcontent.com/pod-product-compliance
Lightning Source LLC
Chambersburg PA
CBHW072154270326
41930CB00011B/2427